Committee for Human Rights in North Korea (HRNK)

Board of Directors

I

ARSENAL OF TERROR

NORTH KOREA, STATE SPONSOR OF TERRORISM

Joshua Stanton

THE COMMITTEE FOR
HUMAN RIGHTS IN NORTH KOREA
북한인권위원회

ISBN: 978-0-9856480-3-9
Library of Congress Control Number: 2015937031

ARSENAL OF TERROR

NORTH KOREA, STATE SPONSOR OF TERRORISM

Committee for Human Rights in North Korea
1001 Connecticut Avenue, NW, Suite 435
Washington, DC 20036
(202) 499-7970
www.hrnk.org

ABOUT THE AUTHOR: JOSHUA STANTON

Joshua Stanton is an attorney in Washington, D.C. with 18 years of military and civilian experience in criminal and civil litigation and administrative law. From 1998 to 2002, he served as a U.S. Army Judge Advocate in the Republic of Korea. In 2006, he testified before the House International Relations Committee. He was the first to identify and publish satellite imagery of three North Korean prison camps, Camp 16 (*Hwasong*), Camp 25 (*Chongjin*), and Camp 12 (*Cheongo-ri*). His work has been cited in *The Wall Street Journal*, *The Washington Post*, *Reuters*, *The Guardian*, and *The Daily Telegraph*, and other sources. His op-eds have been published in *The New York Times*, *The Washington Post, Foreign Policy*, *CNN International*, and *The Weekly Standard*. He recently authored a paper on sanctions against North Korea, which was published in *The Fletcher Security Review*. Since April of 2013, he has assisted the U.S. House of Representatives, Committee on Foreign Affairs, with the drafting of the North Korea Sanctions Enforcement Act of 2014, which passed the full House with 145 co-sponsors, and with H.R. 757, which was introduced in the House on February 5, 2015. The views he expresses are his own and do not represent views of the Foreign Affairs Committee, or of any organization or government agency.

ACKNOWLEDGEMENTS

I offer my sincere gratitude to HRNK Co-Chairs Roberta Cohen and Andrew Natsios, and to all HRNK Board members, with a special thanks to Nicholas Eberstadt, Kevin McCann, Marcus Noland, and Jacqui Pak for their insightful and meticulous comments and edits, and for testing my analysis against their deep reserves of knowledge and judgment. Bruce Bechtol's book, *The Last Days of Kim Jong Il,* was an extremely useful resource for researching North Korea's links to Hezbollah and the Real IRA. Mark Manyin of the Congressional Research Service indulged my pedantic legal arguments with courtesy, patience, and tact. I also wish to thank HRNK staff members Amanda Morwedt Oh, Rosa Park, and Raymond Ha for their work on getting the report ready for publication. The readers of my blog, *One Free Korea,* commented on and tested the first drafts of my arguments over many years. HRNK Executive Director Greg Scarlatoiu honored me by inviting me to contribute this report to HRNK's body of excellent work. Finally, the wife and children I adore allowed me to sequester myself with my laptop for the latter half of my Christmas leave, and for several weekends thereafter, to write this report.

To The Reverend Kim Dong-shik

and to the family that lost him.

TABLE OF CONTENTS

I. EXECUTIVE SUMMARY

Since North Korea's 2008 removal from the list of state sponsors of terrorism, or SSOT, the U.S. State Department's annual Country Reports on Terrorism have each contained an increasingly tendentious and strained assertion: "The Democratic People's Republic of Korea (DPRK) is not known to have sponsored any terrorist acts since the bombing of a Korean Airlines flight in 1987." [1]

Following President Obama's public accusation of North Korea for the 2014 cyberattacks against Sony Pictures Entertainment Inc., and for a threat against audiences of "The Interview," news media have reported that the President is reviewing whether to restore North Korea to the SSOT list. [2] More recently, however, a U.S. State Department spokeswoman suggested that the Obama Administration is leaning against a SSOT re-listing, seeing a re-listing as "symbolic." [3]

This report examines the legal standards for listing a state as a sponsor of terrorism, the legal effects of a SSOT listing, and the evidence that North Korea's recent conduct meets that standard. It finds that the standards are vague and inconsistent, that the U.S. State Department's reporting on terrorism has not always conformed to these standards, that some of the consequences of a SSOT re-listing would be legally and financially significant, and that the evidence of North Korea's recent sponsorship of terrorism is both extensive and consistent with the applicable legal standards and precedents cited to justify previous SSOT listings.

North Korea's sponsorship of terrorism is a threat to human rights in several regions of the world today, including the United States. It involves the sale or transfer of weapons to foreign terrorist organizations. It involves threats to North Korean émigrés and refugees, and South Korean human rights activists, who have become targets for kidnapping and assassination by North Korean agents. More recently, it involves threats to freedom of expression in the United States, and represents a growing threat to the safety of South Korea's civilian population. Although other provocative and even violent conduct by Pyongyang involving South Korea and other countries may not fit the strict legal definitions of international terrorism, it raises concerns related to the sponsorship of terrorism, and calls for appropriate legal options as well.

---

1   U.S. Department of State, Bureau of Counterterrorism, *Country Reports on Terrorism 2013* (April 2014), http://www.state.gov/documents/organization/225886.pdf, 62. This report refers to U.S. State Department annual reports according to the year of the conduct they describe, rather than the year of publication.

2   Amy Chozick, "Obama to See if North Korea Should Return to Terror List," *The New York Times*, 21 December 2014.

3   "U.S. unlikely to re-list N. Korea as state sponsor of terrorism," *Yonhap News*, 23 December 2014.

This report recommends that Congress and the U.S. State Department clarify the legal standards that define state sponsorship of terrorism and consider re-listing North Korea as a SSOT in light of the evidence in this report. It further calls for the creation of alternative remedies for serious threats to international peace that do not meet the legal definition of support for acts of terrorism. And finally, it recommends reconsideration of whether the sanctions associated with a SSOT listing are sufficient to accomplish Congress's purpose in deterring states from sponsoring terrorism.

II. Background

A. Purpose and History of the SSOT List

Congress's purpose for creating the list of state sponsors of terrorism (SSOT) was to deter state sponsorship of terrorism through the threat of sanctions and international isolation. Congress first authorized the Secretary of State to designate countries that have "repeatedly provided support for acts of international terrorism" in the Export Administration Act of 1979. Section 3 of the Act contains the following declaration of policy:

> It is the policy of the United States to use export controls to encourage other countries to take immediate steps to prevent the use of their territories or resources to aid, encourage, or give sanctuary to those persons involved in directing, supporting, or participating in acts of international terrorism. To achieve this objective, the President shall make reasonable and prompt efforts to secure the removal or reduction of such assistance to international terrorists through international cooperation and agreement before imposing export controls.[4]

Amendments to the Foreign Assistance Act of 1961 later conformed its language to that of the Export Administration Act.[5] In 1986, Congress amended the Arms Export Control Act to

---

4   Export Administration Act of 1979, Pub. L. No. 96-72, § 3(8), 93 Stat. 505 (as amended by Pub. L. No. 99-64, § 103(3), 99 Stat. 121).

5   *Compare* International Security Assistance and Arms Export Control Act of 1976, Pub. L. No. 94-329, § 303, 90 Stat. 753 (terminating foreign assistance to "any government which aids or abets, by granting sanctuary from prosecution to, any individual or group which has committed an act of international terrorism"), *with* International Security and Development Cooperation Act of 1985, Pub. L. No. 99-83, § 503, 99 Stat. 220 (incorporating the key language of Section 6(j) of the Export Administration Act into Section 620A of the Foreign Assistance Act).

cross-reference Section 6(j) of the Export Administration Act.[6] In 1996, Congress amended the U.S. Criminal Code to require a license for any transaction with a government listed as a SSOT.[7]

Since 1979, Congress has expanded the deterrent purpose of the SSOT list from bilateral trade sanctions to international isolation of the designated government, if not always consistently. For example, the 1985 amendment to Section 620A of the Foreign Assistance Act urged the President to "call upon other countries to impose similar sanctions on" SSOT-listed governments;[8] however, Congress repealed this provision in 1989.[9] In 1987, Congress passed the Foreign Relations Authorization Act for Fiscal Years 1988 and 1989 (FRAA), requiring the U.S. State Department to report annually on its efforts to disrupt and eliminate terrorist sanctuaries.[10] In Section 2 of the Aviation Security Improvement Act of 1990, Congress found that the United States should "work with other nations to treat as outlaws state sponsors of terrorism, isolating such sponsors politically, economically, and militarily."[11] It called for "a clear understanding that state-sponsored terrorism threatens United States values and interests, and that active measures are needed to counter more effectively the terrorist threat."[12]

Similarly, in Section 324 of the Antiterrorism and Effective Death Penalty Act of 1996, Congress urged the President to "continue to undertake efforts to increase the international isolation of state sponsors of international terrorism, including efforts to strengthen international sanctions."[13]

In its 2008 "Country Reports on Terrorism," the U.S. State Department described the purpose of the SSOT list as follows:

> State sponsors of terrorism provide critical support to non-state
> terrorist groups. Without state sponsors, terrorist groups would have

---

6   Omnibus Diplomatic Security and Antiterrorism Act of 1986, Pub. L. No. 99-399, § 509, 100 Stat. 874.

7   Antiterrorism and Effective Death Penalty Act of 1996, Pub. L. No. 104-132, § 321, 110 Stat. 1254.

8   International Security and Development Cooperation Act of 1985, Pub. L. No. 99-83, § 503, 99 Stat. 220.

9   Anti-Terrorism and Arms Export Amendments Act of 1989, Pub. L. No. 101-222, § 5, 103 Stat. 1897.

10   Foreign Relations Authorization Act, Fiscal Years 1988 and 1989, Pub. L. No. 100-204, § 140, 101 Stat. 1347.

11   Aviation Security Improvement Act of 1990, Pub. L. No. 101-604, § 2(10), 104 Stat. 3067.

12   *Id.* at § 2(11), 104 Stat. 3067.

13   Antiterrorism and Effective Death Penalty Act of 1996, Pub. L. No. 104-132, § 324(6), 110 Stat. 1255.

greater difficulty obtaining the funds, weapons, materials, and secure areas they require to plan and conduct operations. The United States will continue to insist that these countries end the support they give to terrorist groups.[14]

Today, just four states are listed as state sponsors of terrorism: Iran, Syria, Sudan, and Cuba. The U.S. State Department will likely seek to remove Cuba from the SSOT list in 2015.[15]

B. Legal Authority for a SSOT Listing

The principal authority for listing a state as a SSOT is Section 6(j) of the Export Administration Act, which authorizes the Secretary of State to designate governments that "repeatedly provide support for acts of international terrorism." Section 6(j) requires a license to export goods or technology to a country designated as a SSOT, if the "export of such goods or technology could make a significant contribution" to the country's military potential. At least 30 days before issuing such a license, the U.S. Commerce and State Departments must notify their respective congressional oversight committees. Section 6(j) requires no notice before adding a state to the list.[16]

In 2010, in response to a reporter's question about re-listing North Korea as a SSOT, Philip J. Crowley, the Assistant Secretary of the Bureau of Public Affairs, further explained the U.S. State Department's view of the legal criteria for listing:

> The standards for designating a country as a state sponsor and rescinding the designation are set out in the three separate statutes: Section 620A of the Foreign Assistance Act (22 USC 2371), Section 40 of the Arms Export Control Act (22 USC 278), and Section 6(j) of the Export Administration Act (50 USC app 2405(j)). All three statutes provide for the Secretary of State the authority to designate countries the governments of which "repeatedly provide support for acts of international terrorism." Therefore, the Secretary of State must determine that the government of North Korea has repeatedly

14   U.S. Department of State, Office of the Coordinator for Counterterrorism, *Country Reports on Terrorism 2008* (April 2009), http://www.state.gov/documents/organization/122599.pdf, 181.

15   Lesley Wroughton and Mark Hosenball, "Exclusive: U.S. pressing Cuba to restore diplomatic ties before April – officials," *Reuters*, 06 February 2015.

16   Export Administration Act of 1979, Pub. L. No. 96-72, § 6(i), 93 Stat. 515 (as amended).

provided support for acts of international terrorism. The United States will follow the provisions of the law as the facts warrant, and if information exists which indicates that North Korea has repeatedly provided support for acts of terrorism, the Department will take immediate action.[17]

None of the authorities Crowley cited, however, sets forth more detailed criteria for listing a government. Section 6(j) authorizes export controls for countries that the Secretary of State lists, but provides no detailed standard or procedural guidance for listing a government. Section 620A of the Foreign Assistance Act limits foreign assistance to SSOT governments, but does not define "international terrorism" or establish more specific criteria for listing.[18] The third statute Crowley cited, at 22 U.S.C. § 278, turns out to be an authorization to appropriate $2 million to build a laboratory in Panama for the study of tropical diseases.[19] Crowley may have intended to cite 22 U.S.C. § 2780, the code section corresponding to Section 40 of the Arms Export Control Act, which restricts arms exports to states that sponsor terrorism.[20]

None of these statutes defines "international terrorism," or sets specific criteria for listing a state as a sponsor. Instead, they give the Secretary of State complete discretion to add a government to the SSOT list if he finds that the government has "repeatedly provide[d] support for acts of international terrorism."[21]

C. DEFINITIONS OF "INTERNATIONAL TERRORISM" AND "TERRORIST ACTIVITY"

No single statute defines "international terrorism" conclusively for purposes of the SSOT list. To determine whether an act could be considered "international terrorism," one may compare

---

17   U.S. Department of State, "North Korea: State Sponsor of Terrorism? (Taken Question)," last modified 28 June 2010, http://www.state.gov/r/pa/prs/ps/2010/06/143720.htm.

18   Foreign Assistance Act of 1961, Pub. L. No. 87-195, § 620A added by Pub. L. No. 94-329, § 303, 90 Stat. 753 (as amended).

19   Foreign Assistance Act of 1974, Pub. L. No. 93-559, § 47, 88 Stat. 1816 (amending an Act of May 7, 1928, ch. 505, § 1, 45 Stat. 491).

20   International Security Assistance and Arms Export Control Act of 1976, Pub. L. No. 94-329, § 40 added by Pub. L. No. 99-399, § 509(a), 100 Stat. 874 (as amended).

21   U.S. Department of State, Bureau of Counterterrorism, "State Sponsors of Terrorism," http://www.state.gov/j/ct/list/c14151.htm.

a state's conduct to any one of several inconsistent legal definitions, or to the precedent of the U.S. State Department's past annual reporting on terrorism and SSOTs. To confuse matters further, many of these precedents do not fit within one—and in some cases, any—of the statutory definitions. Collectively, however, these definitions and precedents allow one to form an imprecise operational definition of "international terrorism."

The U.S. State Department has long noted the lack of a single accepted legal definition of terrorism,[22] but has sometimes cited the definition found at Section 140 of the Foreign Relations Authorization Act for Fiscal Years 1988 and 1989, codified at 22 U.S.C. § 2656f (FRAA Section 140). This provision requires the U.S. State Department to publish annual reports on patterns of global terrorism. This section defines "international terrorism" as "terrorism involving the citizens or the territory of more than 1 country," and defines "terrorism" as "premeditated, politically motivated violence perpetrated against noncombatant targets by subnational groups or clandestine agents." This definition does not further define "violence," nor does it clarify that threats of violence fall within the definition of international terrorism.[23]

Section 6(j) of the Export Administration Act neither cites this definition nor provides an alternative definition, raising the question of whether this language defines "international terrorism" for purposes of the SSOT list.[24] The U.S. State Department's 2005 "Country Report on Terrorism" notes that the FRAA Section 140 definition is just "one of many US statutes and international legal instruments that concern terrorism and acts of violence, many of which use definitions for terrorism and related terms that are different from those used in this report."[25]

The U.S. Criminal Code contains a more precise definition of "international terrorism" at 18 U.S.C. § 2331(1). This definition includes violent or dangerous acts, committed outside the United States or across international boundaries, that would be crimes if committed in the United States, and which appear to be intended to intimidate or coerce a government or a civilian population, to influence a government's policies through intimidation or coercion, or to

---

22   *See* U.S. Department of State, Office of the Ambassador-at-Large for Counterterrorism, *Patterns of Global Terrorism: 1988* (April 1989), http://www.higginsctc.org/patternsofglobalterrorism/1988pogt.pdf, v.

23   Foreign Relations Authorization Act, Fiscal Years 1988 and 1989, Pub. L. No. 100-204, § 140(d), 101 Stat. 1349 (as amended).

24   Export Administration Act of 1979, Pub. L. No. 96-72, § 6(i), 93 Stat. 515 (as amended).

25   U.S. Department of State, Office of the Coordinator for Counterterrorism, *Country Reports on Terrorism 2005* (April 2006), http://www.state.gov/documents/organization/65462.pdf, 9.

affect the conduct of a government by mass destruction, assassination, or kidnapping. Another section of the same chapter, Section 2332b(c), provides that attempts to commit terrorist acts are punishable to the same extent as completed acts of terrorism, and that threats to commit terrorist acts are punishable by ten years in prison.

The Treasury Department applies another definition of "terrorism" for purposes of Executive Order 13,224, an authority under the International Emergency Economic Powers Act that allows Treasury to block the assets and property of persons and entities engaging in, or providing material support for, terrorism.[26] This executive order defines "terrorism" as "an activity that … involves a violent act or an act dangerous to human life, property, or infrastructure; and [that] appears to be intended to intimidate or coerce a civilian population; to influence the policy of a government by intimidation or coercion; or to affect the conduct of a government by mass destruction, assassination, kidnapping, or hostage-taking."[27] This language is therefore similar to the Criminal Code's definition of "international terrorism."

The Immigration and Nationality Act (INA) defines yet another term, "terrorist activity," at Section 212(a)(3)(B)(iii):[28]

(iii) "Terrorist Activity" defined

As used in this chapter, the term "terrorist activity" means any activity which is unlawful under the laws of the place where it is committed (or which, if it had been committed in the United States, would be unlawful under the laws of the United States or any State) and which involves any of the following:

(I) The highjacking or sabotage of any conveyance (including an aircraft, vessel, or vehicle).

(II) The seizing or detaining, and threatening to kill, injure, or continue to detain, another individual in order to compel a third person (including a governmental organization) to do or

---

26   International Emergency Economic Powers Act, Pub. L. No. 95-223, 91 Stat. 1626 (as amended).

27   Exec. Order No. 13,224, 66 Fed. Reg. 49079 (Sep. 25, 2001).

28   Immigration and Nationality Act, Pub. L. No. 82-414, § 212(a)(3)(B)(ii) added by Pub. L. No. 101-649, § 601(a), 104 Stat. 5067 (as amended by Pub. L. No. 107-56, § 411(a)(1), 115 Stat. 345).

abstain from doing any act as an explicit or implicit condition for the release of the individual seized or detained.

(III) A violent attack upon an internationally protected person (as defined in section 1116(b)(4) of title 18) or upon the liberty of such a person.[29]

(IV) An assassination.

(V) The use of any—

(a) biological agent, chemical agent, or nuclear weapon or device, or

(b) explosive, firearm, or other weapon or dangerous device (other than for mere personal monetary gain), with intent to endanger, directly or indirectly, the safety of one or more individuals or to cause substantial damage to property.

(VI) A threat, attempt, or conspiracy to do any of the foregoing.

The U.S. State Department uses this definition and the definition of "terrorism" at FRAA Section 140, as standards for its designation of Foreign Terrorist Organizations.[30] Because the INA and FRAA definitions are both recognized in how the U.S. State Department defines terrorism—admittedly, in slightly different contexts—this report applies both definitions. It also refers to the

---

29   Under 18 U.S.C. § 1116(b)(4), the term "internationally protected person" means—

(A) a Chief of State or the political equivalent, head of government, or Foreign Minister whenever such person is in a country other than his own and any member of his family accompanying him; or

(B) any other representative, officer, employee, or agent of the United States Government, a foreign government, or international organization who at the time and place concerned is entitled pursuant to international law to special protection against attack upon his person, freedom, or dignity, and any member of his family then forming part of his household.

30   U.S. Department of State, Bureau of Counterterrorism, "Foreign Terrorist Organizations: Legal Criteria for Designation under Section 219 of the INA as amended," http://www.state.gov/j/ct/rls/other/des/123085.htm.

Criminal Code and Executive Order 13,224 definitions of "international terrorism" when they are instructive.

D. Definition of "Support"

Section 6(j)(5) of the Export Administration Act defines "repeatedly provid[ing] support" to include "expressly consent[ing] to" or tolerating the provision of sanctuary to terrorists, but does not specify what other conduct could also constitute support for terrorism.[31]

A 1989 Congressional report provides a more coherent operational definition of "support," listing the following seven categories of conduct:[32]

- allowing a country's territory to be used as a sanctuary;

- furnishing lethal substances to individuals or groups with the likelihood that they will be used for terrorism;

- providing logistical support to terrorists or terrorist groups;

- providing safe haven or headquarters for terrorists or terrorist organizations;

- planning, directing, training or assisting in the execution of terrorist activities;

- providing direct or indirect financial support for terrorist activities; and

- providing diplomatic facilities such as support or documentation to aid or abet terrorist activities.

The Congressional Research Service has cited this report as "provid[ing] guidelines for designation," but the report is not positive law and does not bind the executive branch.[33] Neither set of

---

31   Export Administration Act of 1979, Pub. L. No. 96-72, § 6(j)(5) added by Pub. L. No. 108-458, § 7102(c)(1), 118 Stat. 3776.

32   U.S. House Committee on Foreign Affairs. *Anti-Terrorism and Arms Export Amendments Act of 1989: report (to Accompany H.R. 91).* (101 H. Rpt. 296).

33   Larry Niksch and Raphael Perl, "North Korea: Terrorism List Removal?," *CRS Report for Congress RL30613* (06 April 2007), http://assets.opencrs.com/rpts/RL30613_20070406.pdf, 11.

criteria answers other important questions, such as whether "support for acts of international terrorism" includes only indirect support, or also includes a state's direction of, or participation in, acts of terrorism.

Section 212(a)(3)(B)(iv) of the Immigration and Nationality Act defines "engage in terrorist activity" to include a variety of supporting conduct, including inciting, planning, or preparing terrorist attacks, soliciting funds for terrorist organizations, gathering information for targeting, or providing material support for terrorists.[34]

Finally, the U.S. State Department's annual country reports on terrorism constitute a collection of historical precedents for the applied definitions of "international terrorism" and "support."

E. Conduct Supporting Prior SSOT Listings

Since at least 1976, the Central Intelligence Agency and the U.S. State Department have published detailed annual reports on global terrorism.[35] On December 22, 1987, President Reagan signed the FRAA. Section 140 of the FRAA requires the U.S. State Department to publish annual, country-specific reports on terrorist activity and state sponsorship of terrorism.

Although substantially similar in structure and content, these annual reports have been published under three different names—"Patterns of International Terrorism" until 1982, "Patterns of Global Terrorism" from 1983 to 2003, and "Country Reports on Terrorism" since 2004. These reports describe the reasons for each state's continued listing, and provide insight into the criteria for listing in practice.

FRAA Section 140 does not explicitly define "support," but requires the U.S. State Department to report on several categories of conduct in its annual reports on terrorism:[36]

- For any country "in which acts of international terrorism ... of major significance" have occurred, which the Secretary of State has designated as a SSOT and notified Congress

---

34 Immigration and Nationality Act, Pub. L. No. 82-414, § 212(a)(3)(B)(iii) added by Pub. L. No. 101-649, § 601(a), 104 Stat. 5067 (as amended).

35 Annual reports issued between 1976 and 2003 can be accessed at http://www.higginsctc.org/patternsofglobalterrorism.php.

36 Foreign Relations Authorization Act, Fiscal Years 1988 and 1989, Pub. L. No. 100-204, § 140, 101 Stat. 1347 (as amended).

regarding an export under Section 6(j) of the Export Administration Act, and "which the Secretary determines should be the subject of such report," the U.S. State Department must report on that government's major counterterrorism efforts, and its significant political, financial, diplomatic, and material support for terrorism.

- For countries "whose territory is being used as a sanctuary for terrorists or terrorist organizations," the U.S. State Department must report on the extent of the government's knowledge of terrorist activities on its territory, its efforts to eliminate terrorist sanctuaries on its territory and cooperate with U.S. anti-terrorism efforts, and its efforts "to prevent the proliferation of and trafficking in weapons of mass destruction in and through the territory of the country."

- For any terrorist group "known to be financed by" SSOT-listed governments, the U.S. State Department must report on the government's significant financial support to the group, its efforts to deprive the group of financial support, and its provision of training, weapons, diplomatic support, and sanctuary to the terrorist group.

- For countries from which the U.S. Government has sought cooperation during the previous five years, the U.S. State Department must report on the extent of those countries' cooperation with U.S. anti-terrorism efforts.

It is not clear that Congress intended for these overlapping and underlapping requirements to constitute an operational definition of "support for acts of international terrorism." They do not clearly require the U.S. State Department to summarize the support for international terrorism each SSOT-listed government provides each year. In some regards, they are under-inclusive for this purpose; for example, they would not require the U.S. State Department to report on support for terrorism by an SSOT-listed government for which the Secretary of State did *not* notify Congress of an export under Section 6(j) of the Export Administration Act. In other regards, they would be over-inclusive; for example, they would require the Secretary of State to report that a non-SSOT-listed government, whose territory was being used as a sanctuary by terrorists,[37] had proliferated weapons of mass destruction to another government, regardless of whether the receiving government was SSOT listed.

Historically, the relationship between these legal standards and SSOT listings has been fluid. The standards, and the manner in which the U.S. State Department has applied them, have been malleable enough to conform to the shifting policy considerations that appear to drive them. The U.S.

---

37   North Korea, which continues to harbor four Japanese Red Army hijackers, is an example of such a government.

State Department's annual "Country Reports" have frequently cited conduct that does not fit the legal definitions of terrorism or FRAA reporting requirements, such as inadequate legal counter-measures against terrorist financing and diplomatic relationships among SSOT governments.

Conversely, conduct that the U.S. State Department has not cited (such as North Korea's assassinations of activists and émigrés, or its weapons sales to the Tamil Tigers and Hezbollah, *infra* Section IV.A.4) often seems more provocative and dangerous than the conduct it has cited (such as meetings between Iranian and Syrian government officials; *infra* Section II.E.7). Eventually, this flexibility would allow the U.S. State Department to remove North Korea from the SSOT list, and to keep it off the list, despite Pyongyang's repeated sponsorship of acts of international terrorism (*infra* Sections IV and V).

One conclusion that emerges from the U.S. State Department's annual reporting is that the U.S. State Department considers both acts of terrorism by a state and a state's support for any terrorist organization to be justifications for an SSOT listing. Thus, the precedent strongly suggests that "support for" and "acts of international terrorism" should be read as disjunctive, rather than conjunctive criteria for listing. The congressional report cited in Section II.D helps to harmonize this distinction by specifying that state sponsorship of terrorism includes "planning, directing, training or assisting in the execution of terrorist activities."

1. SPONSORSHIP OF TERRORIST ORGANIZATIONS

The most obvious basis for a SSOT listing is material support for non-state terrorist actors, such as those the U.S. State Department cited in support of Iran's listing in its 2012 annual terrorism report. The same report also cited Cuba, Iran, and Syria for their material support to terrorist groups, and Iran and Cuba for harboring fugitive terrorists.[38]

The U.S. State Department maintains a list of designated Foreign Terrorist Organizations.[39] Separately, the Treasury Department also sanctions individual terrorists and terrorist organizations under Executive Order 13,224. The U.S. State and Treasury Department lists overlap but do not match, and the U.S. State Department's annual terrorism reports may refer to acts of terrorism by, or the sponsorship of, organizations that appear on only one of the lists, or neither one.

---

38   U.S. Department of State, Office of the Coordinator for Counterterrorism, *Country Reports on Terrorism 2012* (May 2013), http://www.state.gov/documents/organization/210204.pdf, 195-97, 199-200.

39   U.S. Department of State, Bureau of Counterterrorism, "Foreign Terrorist Organizations," http://www.state.gov/j/ct/rls/other/des/123085.htm.

For example, the U.S. State Department has repeatedly cited North Korea's harboring of Japanese Red Army terrorists both before and after the period between 1997 and 2001, when the Japanese Red Army was designated as a Foreign Terrorist Organization. The U.S. State Department's 2005,[40] 2007,[41] 2010,[42] 2012,[43] and 2013 "Country Reports"[44] all cited Iran and Syria for supplying weapons to Hezbollah through Syrian territory. Most of these reports also cited Iran's training of Hezbollah. Most directly relevant to this report, however, is this passage from the U.S. State Department's 2009 "Country Reports," regarding Syria's state sponsorship of Hezbollah:

> Underscoring links between the Syrian government and Hizballah, Israeli naval commandos intercepted a large cache of arms on November 3 on its way from Iran to Hizballah by way of the Syrian port of Latakia. The arms shipment, which was found amidst civilian cargo on the Antiguan-flagged ship MV Francop, weighed over 500 tons. While the Syrian government denied involvement in the shipment, Israeli officials stressed that the incident illustrates Syria's continued efforts to fight a proxy war with Israel through terrorist groups like Hizballah. The last attack across the internationally-recognized Israeli line of withdrawal (a.k.a. the Blue Line) occurred in 2006.[45]

In March 2014, a UN Panel of Experts (UN POE) determined that the weapons in this shipment were of North Korean origin (*infra* Section IV.A.2). The U.S. State Department has never acknowledged North Korea's role in this incident, or in a series of weapons seizures described in Section IV.C of this report.

---

40   U.S. Department of State, *Country Reports on Terrorism 2005*, 173, 176-77.

41   U.S. Department of State, Office of the Coordinator for Counterterrorism, *Country Reports on Terrorism 2007* (April 2008), http://www.state.gov/documents/organization/105904.pdf, 172-73, 174-76.

42   U.S. Department of State, Office of the Coordinator for Counterterrorism, *Country Reports on Terrorism 2010* (August 2011), http://www.state.gov/documents/organization/170479.pdf, 150-53.

43   U.S. Department of State, *Country Reports on Terrorism 2012*, 196-97, 199-200.

44   U.S. Department of State, *Country Reports on Terrorism 2013*, 228-32.

45   U.S. Department of State, Office of the Coordinator for Counterterrorism, *Country Reports on Terrorism 2009* (August 2010), http://www.state.gov/documents/organization/141114.pdf, 195.

2. TERRORISM BY STATE ACTORS

The U.S. State Department has frequently cited the actions of the intelligence and uniformed services of foreign governments—including North Korea's—in its reporting on the state sponsorship of terrorism. In each of these cases, the state actors were operating abroad in a clandestine capacity.

In 1983, North Korean officers placed a bomb at the Martyrs' Mausoleum in Rangoon (*infra* Section III.B).[46] The bomb missed its primary target, South Korean President Chun Doo-hwan, but killed 21 people, including 13 senior South Korean officials and two members of the Presidential Guard.[47] The U.S. State Department described the bombing as a terrorist attack,[48, 49] but did not list North Korea as a SSOT until 1988, after two North Korean intelligence officers bombed Korean Air Lines Flight 858 (*infra* Section III.C). The U.S. State Department later confirmed that North Korea was listed as an SSOT "because of its responsibility for the November 1987 destruction of a South Korean airliner and the 1983 terrorist attack against Republic of Korea officials in Rangoon, Burma."[50] Both attacks have been attributed to officers of North Korea's Reconnaissance General Bureau (RGB), a uniformed intelligence service that carries out most of North Korea's clandestine foreign operations (*infra* Section II.E.6).[51]

The U.S. State Department's citation of the RGB's acts is consistent with its previous citations of acts by the clandestine services of the Iranian, Iraqi, and Libyan governments, particularly Iran's Quds Force. The Quds Force is a branch of the Islamic Revolutionary Guard Corps (IRGC) and an organization of the Iranian government that performs military, paramilitary, and intelligence

---

46   "North Korean Reported To Confess in Burma," *Associated Press*, 24 November 1983.

47   Clyde Haberman, "Bomb Kills 19, Including 6 Key Koreans," *The New York Times*, 10 October 1983.

48   U.S. Department of State, *Patterns of Global Terrorism: 1983* (September 1984), http://www.higginsctc.org/patternsofglobalterrorism/1983PoGT.pdf, 19.

49   For more discussion of this subject, see Jennifer Elsea, "Terrorism and the Law of War: Trying Terrorists as War Criminals before Military Commissions," *CRS Report for Congress RL31191* (11 December 2001), http://fas.org/irp/crs/RL31191.pdf.

50   U.S. Department of State, Office of the Coordinator for Counter-Terrorism, *Patterns of Global Terrorism: 1989* (April 1990), http://www.higginsctc.org/patternsofglobalterrorism/1989pogt.pdf, 47.

51   Joseph S. Bermudez Jr., "Special Report 4: A New Emphasis on Operations Against South Korea? A Guide to North Korea's Intelligence Reorganization and the General Reconnaissance Bureau," *38 North* (11 June 2010), http://38north.org/wp-content/uploads/2010/06/38north_SR_Bermudez2.pdf, 8-9.

functions. The U.S. State Department has repeatedly accused the Quds Force of sponsoring Foreign Terrorist Organizations, including Hezbollah, and of directly plotting and carrying out terrorist attacks using IGRC-QF personnel. In its 2009 report, the U.S. State Department cited the indictment by Argentinian authorities of "[s]enior IRGC, IRGC Qods Force, and Iranian government officials" for "their alleged roles in the 1994 terrorist bombing of the Argentine-Jewish Mutual Association," which killed 85 people and injured several hundred others. The report notes that "according to the Argentine State Prosecutor's report, the attack was initially proposed by the Quds Force," and that INTERPOL consequently issued a "red notice" for "Ahmad Vahidi, who was named as Iran's Defense Minister in August 2009."[52]

The U.S. State Department's 2012 report cites the guilty plea of a Quds Force agent in a plot to murder the Saudi Ambassador to the United States on U.S. soil, and states that a second indicted co-conspirator, a Quds Force officer, remains at large. It also cites the 2012 arrest of two Quds Force officers in Kenya, who allegedly stockpiled explosives for a terrorist attack.[53]

The U.S. State Department has also cited actions of Syrian government agents, including their suspected involvement in the February 2005 assassination of former Lebanese Prime Minister Rafiq Hariri.[54]

The U.S. State Department and the Treasury Department differ in their willingness to designate state actors as terrorist organizations. Although the U.S. State Department has repeatedly cited terrorist acts by the Quds Force in its reporting on Iran's state sponsorship of terrorism, it has not designated the Quds Force as a Foreign Terrorist Organization.[55] The apparent reason for this is a policy-based hesitation to designate state actors.[56] This is true notwithstanding the fact that the Quds Force appears to meet the U.S. State Department's legal criteria for designation:[57]

---

52   U.S. Department of State, *Country Reports on Terrorism 2009*, 193.

53   U.S. Department of State, *Country Reports on Terrorism 2012*, 196.

54   U.S. Department of State, *Country Reports on Terrorism 2008*, 185.

55   U.S. Department of State, Bureau of Counterterrorism, "Foreign Terrorist Organizations: Legal Criteria for Designation under Section 219 of the INA as amended," http://www.state.gov/j/ct/rls/other/des/123085.htm.

56   Patrick Goodenough, "House Bill Would Designate Iran's Revolutionary Guard As Terrorist Group," *CNS News*, 28 February 2013.

57   U.S. Department of State, Bureau of Counterterrorism, "Foreign Terrorist Organizations," http://www.state.gov/j/ct/rls/other/des/123085.htm.

it is a foreign organization; it engages in terrorist activity;[58] and its activity threatens the security of U.S. nationals or the national security of the United States.[59]

The Treasury Department, by contrast, has designated the Quds Force under Executive Order 13,224 for its support for Foreign Terrorist Organizations, including its provision of weapons and training to Hezbollah.[60] According to *The Washington Post*, the Quds Force was "the first national military branch included" on Treasury's list of groups designated under the executive order, calling this "a highly unusual move because it is part of a government, rather than a typical non-state terrorist organization."[61]

3. THREATS AND ATTEMPTS

Although the Section 140 definition of "international terrorism" does not specifically include threats or attempts, the INA 212 definition of "terrorist activity" includes both, and U.S. State Department reports have repeatedly described threats as acts of terrorism. For example, State's 2013 "Country Reports" cites a threat by an anarchist group to poison soft drinks,[62] the conviction by a Norwegian court of an Ansar-al-Islam leader for "issuing threats and intimidating witnesses,"[63] a bomb threat by Aum Shinrikyo,[64] a death threat by Harakat-al-Mujaheddin,[65] a threat by

---

58   *Id*. The U.S. State Department cites the definitions "in section 212 (a)(3)(B) of the INA (8 U.S.C. § 1182(a)(3)(B)), or terrorism, as defined in section 140(d)(2) of the Foreign Relations Authorization Act, Fiscal Years 1988 and 1989 (22 U.S.C. § 2656f(d)(2))."

59   *Id*. "National security" includes the "national defense, foreign relations, or the economic interests" of the United States.

60   U.S. Department of the Treasury, "Fact Sheet: Designation of Iranian Entities and Individuals for Proliferation Activities and Support for Terrorism," 25 October 2007, http://www.treasury.gov/press-center/press-releases/Pages/hp644.aspx.

61   Robin Wright, "Iranian Unit to Be Labeled 'Terrorist'," *The Washington Post*, 15 August 2007.

62   U.S. Department of State, *Country Reports on Terrorism 2013*, 96.

63   *Id*. at 271.

64   *Id*. at 273.

65   *Id*. at 282.

Jaish-e-Mohammed against an Indian politician,[66] and threats by the Jewish extremiza-tion Kahane Chai.[67]

The U.S. State Department has also cited threats by state actors, including a threat by Iran against Saudi Arabia (1989),[68] Iraqi threats against Saudi interests (1990),[69] Iranian threats that participants in the Middle East peace process would "suffer the wrath of nations" (1991),[70] Libyan threats to support extremists in neighboring countries (1993),[71] Libyan threats against dissidents abroad (1994,[72] 1997,[73] and 1998[74]), and alleged attempts by the former Iraqi regime to intimidate dissidents abroad (2000[75] and 2002[76]), including by arresting their relatives in Iraq.

---

66   *Id.* at 288.

67   *Id.* at 291.

68   U.S. Department of State, *Patterns of Global Terrorism: 1989*, 15.

69   U.S. Department of State, Office of the Coordinator for Counter-Terrorism, *Patterns of Global Terrorism: 1990* (April 1991), http://www.higginsctc.org/patternsofglobalterrorism/1990pogt.pdf, 29, 31.

70   U.S. Department of State, Office of the Coordinator for Counterterrorism, *Patterns of Global Terrorism: 1991* (April 1992), http://www.higginsctc.org/patternsofglobalterrorism/1991pogt.pdf, 31.

71   U.S. Department of State, Office of the Coordinator for Counterterrorism, *Patterns of Global Terrorism: 1993* (April 1994), http://www.higginsctc.org/patternsofglobalterrorism/1993POGT.pdf, 24.

72   U.S. Department of State, Office of the Coordinator for Counterterrorism, *Patterns of Global Terrorism: 1994* (April 1995), http://www.higginsctc.org/patternsofglobalterrorism/1994pogt.pdf, 22-23.

73   U.S. Department of State, Office of the Coordinator for Counterterrorism, "Overview of State-Sponsored Terrorism: Libya," in *Patterns of Global Terrorism: 1997* (April 1998), http://www.state.gov/www/global/terror-ism/1997Report/1997index.html.

74   U.S. Department of State, Office of the Coordinator for Counterterrorism, "Overview of State-Sponsored Terrorism: Libya," in *Patterns of Global Terrorism: 1998* (April 1999), http://www.state.gov/www/global/terror-ism/1998Report/1998index.html.

75   U.S. Department of State, Office of the Coordinator for Counterterrorism, "Overview of State-Sponsored Terrorism: Iraq," in *Patterns of Global Terrorism: 2000* (April 2001), http://www.state.gov/j/ct/rls/crt/2000/.

76   U.S. Department of State, Office of the Coordinator for Counterterrorism, *Patterns of Global Terrorism: 2002* (April 2003), http://www.state.gov/documents/organization/20177.pdf, 79.

U.S. State Department reports have also cited attempts as terrorist attacks, including Iraq's attempt to kill former President George H.W. Bush (1993)[77] and Iran's attempt to assassinate the Saudi Ambassador to the United States (2011).[78]

In recent years, the U.S. State Department has not cited threats by state actors, including North Korea. Because the U.S. State Department applies the FRAA Section 140 definition of "international terrorism" (among others) to state and non-state actors, this shift does not suggest that the U.S. State Department's interpretation of the definition of this term has evolved. It may reflect a policy choice by the U.S. State Department, the evolving methods of the remaining SSOT governments, or a decline in the number of listed state sponsors following the overthrow of the Iraqi and Libyan governments. In recent years, however, the U.S. State Department has cited Syria for allowing Iraqi extremists to broadcast "violent messages in support of terrorism" into Iraq (2009,[79] 2010,[80] and 2012[81]).

4. ATTACKS AGAINST DISSIDENTS ABROAD

The U.S. State Department has frequently cited plots and attacks by foreign intelligence services against dissidents abroad in its reporting on the state sponsorship of terrorism. As early as 1989, the U.S. State Department accused Iran of "assassinating at least five Iranian dissidents."[82] In 1994, the U.S. State Department's reporting on Iran's state sponsorship of terrorism cited the assassination of a dissident in Turkey, the wounding of a dissident by a letter bomb, the killing of three dissidents in Iraq, the assassination of two other dissidents in Copenhagen and Bucharest, and France's conviction of three Iranians (including a nephew of the Ayatollah Khomeini) for the 1991 murder of a former Prime Minister and his assistant.[83]

---

77   U.S. Department of State, *Patterns of Global Terrorism: 1993*, 23.

78   U.S. Department of State, Bureau of Counterterrorism, *Country Reports on Terrorism 2011* (July 2012), http://www.state.gov/documents/organization/195768.pdf, 6.

79   U.S. Department of State, *Country Reports on Terrorism 2009*, 196.

80   U.S. Department of State, *Country Reports on Terrorism 2010*, 152.

81   U.S. Department of State, *Country Reports on Terrorism 2011*, 174.

82   U.S. Department of State, *Country Reports on Terrorism 1989*, 46.

83   U.S. Department of State, *Patterns of Global Terrorism: 1994*, 21.

The U.S. State Department's 1994 report also cited Iraq's assassination of a dissident in Beirut, for which Lebanon implicated the Iraqi government, arrested two Iraqi diplomats, and severed diplomatic relations with Iraq.[84] It also cited Libya's suspected involvement in the disappearance of a dissident and human rights activist in Egypt.[85] The U.S. State Department's 1997 report alleged that the Libyan government executed the activist in early 1994.[86]

The U.S. State Department's 1995 report accused Iran of escalating "its assassination campaign against dissidents living abroad," voicing suspicions that Iran was involved in the murders of seven dissidents in Iraq, France, and Denmark.[87] The following year, the U.S. State Department accused Iran of "at least eight dissident assassinations outside Iran," including the assassination in Paris of a former government official "by an Iranian resident of Germany with alleged ties to Iran's Ministry of Intelligence and Security (MOIS)."[88] Its 1996 report noted that German authorities had issued an arrest warrant for Iran's Intelligence Minister for ordering the 1992 assassinations of four Iranian-Kurdish dissidents in a Berlin restaurant.[89] According to the U.S. State Department's 1997 "Country Reports," the German court found that "the Government of Iran had followed a deliberate policy of liquidating the regime's opponents who lived outside Iran," and that the assassinations "had been approved at the most senior levels of the Iranian Government," including by "the Minister of Intelligence and Security, the Foreign Minister, the President, and the Supreme Leader."[90] The U.S. State Department's 1998[91] and 1999[92] reports made similar allegations.

---

84   *Id.* at 14.

85   *Id.* at 19-20.

86   U.S. Department of State, "Overview of State-Sponsored Terrorism: Libya," in *Patterns of Global Terrorism: 1997*.

87   U.S. Department of State, Office of the Coordinator for Counterterrorism, *Patterns of Global Terrorism: 1995* (April 1996), http://www.higginsctc.org/patternsofglobalterrorism/1995pogt.pdf, 24.

88   U.S. Department of State, Office of the Coordinator for Counterterrorism, "Overview of State-Sponsored Terrorism: Iran," in *Patterns of Global Terrorism: 1996*, http://www.state.gov/www/global/terrorism/1996Report/1996index.html.

89   *Id.*

90   U.S. Department of State, "Overview of State-Sponsored Terrorism: Iran," in *Patterns of Global Terrorism: 1997*.

91   U.S. Department of State, "Overview of State-Sponsored Terrorism: Iran," in *Patterns of Global Terrorism: 1998*.

92   U.S. Department of State, Office of the Coordinator for Counterterrorism, *Patterns of Global Terrorism: 1999* (April 2000), http://www.state.gov/www/global/terrorism/1999report/patterns.pdf, 56.

In 2000[93] and 2001,[94] the U.S. State Department accused the Iraqi Intelligence Service of collecting intelligence on, and attempting to intimidate, dissident groups abroad. Its 2002[95] report accused Iraqi Intelligence of assassinating another dissident in Lebanon.[96]

5. Terrorism Directed against Military Targets

The U.S. State Department has sometimes classified attacks against military targets not presently engaged in hostilities—such as the attacks on Khobar Towers,[97] the Beirut Marine Barracks,[98] and the Pentagon[99]—as acts of terrorism. All of these were attacks by non-state actors against military personnel not presently engaged in combat operations. The U.S. State Department has distinguished terrorist attacks from acts of war according to the duty status of the targeted personnel. In its 2003 "Country Reports," for example, the U.S. State Department distinguished attacks "directed at combatants … on duty" from attacks against "military personnel who at the time of the incident were unarmed and/or not on duty."[100]

---

93   U.S. Department of State, "Overview of State-Sponsored Terrorism: Iraq," in *Patterns of Global Terrorism: 2000.*

94   U.S. Department of State, Office of the Coordinator for Counterterrorism, *Patterns of Global Terrorism: 2001 (May 2002)*, http://www.state.gov/documents/organization/10319.pdf, 65, 67.

95   U.S. Department of State, *Patterns of Global Terrorism: 2002*, 79.

96   Whether to classify the actions of a state as terrorism is a matter of some controversy among other governments. *See* the Report of the Secretary General's High-level Panel on Threats, Challenges and Change, para. 160, U.N. Doc. A/59/565 (2004) at http://www.un.org/Docs/journal/asp/ws.asp?m=A/59/565:

> The search for an agreed definition usually stumbles on two issues. The first is the argument that any definition should include States' use of armed forces against civilians. We believe that the legal and normative framework against State violations is far stronger than in the case of non-State actors and we do not find this objection to be compelling.

97   U.S. Department of State, "Introduction," in *Patterns of Global Terrorism: 1996.*

98   U.S. Department of State, *Patterns of Global Terrorism: 1983*, 4.

99   U.S. Department of State, *Patterns of Global Terrorism: 2001*, 1.

100   U.S. Department of State, Office of the Coordinator for Counterterrorism, *Patterns of Global Terrorism: 2003 (April 2004)*, http://www.state.gov/documents/organization/31912.pdf, vii.

6. THE RECONNAISSANCE GENERAL BUREAU

Most of North Korea's violent attacks on foreign soil have been the work of the Reconnaissance General Bureau of the Workers' Party of Korea, also known as the RGB, or Unit 586. The RGB is a uniformed intelligence service of the North Korean government. According to analyst and author Joseph Bermudez, the RGB is divided into several bureaus, some of which have been involved in activities associated with terrorism.

According to Bermudez, the First Bureau of the RGB has "been involved in kidnapping operations throughout the world intended to secure persons to serve as language and cultural instructors for North Korean operatives," including in Japan, using "a wide variety of specialized swimmer delivery vehicles, semi-submersible infiltration landing craft, infiltration vessels and midget and coastal-submarines." It has also earned foreign currency through illicit activities, including currency counterfeiting.[101]

The RGB's Second Bureau "has been responsible for numerous anti-ROK operations over the years," including the January 1968 attack on the South Korea's presidential palace, the 1983 Rangoon bombing (*infra* Section III.B); the 2010 attempt to assassinate former Korean Workers' Party Secretary Hwang Jang-yop in Seoul (*infra* Section IV.B.2); and the 2010 sinking of the South Korean Navy corvette *Cheonan* (*infra* Section V.C.1). The Second Bureau is also believed to be responsible for providing weapons and training to foreign entities (*infra* Section IV.A), including terrorist groups.[102]

The RGB's Fifth Bureau primarily gathers intelligence on targets in South Korea, including North Korean refugees.[103]

Bermudez also asserts that senior RGB officials were involved in the 1987 bombing of Korean Airlines flight 858 (*infra* Section III.C).[104] In 2010, Bermudez described a reorganization and consolidation of the RGB, and wrote that the reorganization suggested that Pyongyang "may be adopting an active policy against South Korea that may include more provocative operations in the future."[105]

---

101   Joseph S. Bermudez Jr., "Special Report 4: A New Emphasis on Operations Against South Korea?," *38 North*, 7.

102   *Id.* at 8-9.

103   *Id.* at 9.

104   *Id.*

105   *Id.* at 2.

The RGB is also believed to oversee the operations of Unit 121,[106] the North Korean computer hacking unit that the Federal Bureau of Investigation (FBI) suspects of carrying out the 2014 cyberattacks against Sony Pictures Entertainment Inc.[107] and the threats against audiences of "The Interview."[108] On January 2, 2015, President Obama designated the RGB and two other entities under Executive Order 13,687. The executive order cited "the provocative, destabilizing, and repressive actions and policies of the Government of North Korea, including its destructive, coercive cyber-related actions during November and December 2014" and its "commission of serious human rights abuses."[109] In 2010, the President had previously designated the RGB under Executive Order 13,551, for its involvement in the proliferation of weapons of mass destruction.[110]

Thus, the RGB's role in North Korea's foreign clandestine operations is analogous to that of Iran's Quds Force.

[Satellite image of RGB facility north of Pyongyang, via NKEconWatch.com[111]]

---

106   Ju-min Park and James Pearson, "In North Korea, hackers are a handpicked, pampered elite," *Reuters*, 05 December 2014.

107   Federal Bureau of Investigation, "Update on Sony Investigation," 19 December 2014, http://www.fbi.gov/news/pressrel/press-releases/update-on-sony-investigation.

108   David E. Sanger and Martin Fackler, "N.S.A. Breached North Korean Networks Before Sony Attack, Officials Say," *The New York Times*, 18 January 2015.

109   Exec. Order No. 13,687, 80 Fed. Reg. 817 (Jan. 06, 2015).

110   Exec. Order No. 13,551, 75 Fed. Reg. 53837 (Sep. 01, 2010).

111   "KPA Reconnaissance Bureau (Unit 586) located," *North Korea Economy Watch*, 28 April 2010, http://www.nkeconwatch.com/2010/04/28/kpa-reconnaissance-bureau-located/.

7. OTHER CONDUCT CITED

Not all of the categories of conduct the U.S. State Department has cited in its country reports on the state sponsorship of terrorism fit within the definitions of "support," "international terrorism," or "terrorist activity." The U.S. State Department's reporting of this conduct has sometimes exceeded the reporting requirements of FRAA Section 140. The U.S. State Department may have reported this conduct in accordance with other policy considerations to support a government's SSOT listing.

For example, State has cited Iran, Syria, and North Korea for concerns about proliferation of nuclear and chemical weapons, and ballistic missiles. In explaining its rationale for including this conduct in its annual reporting, the State Department said the following:

> State sponsors of terrorism provide critical support to non-state terrorist groups. Without state sponsors, terrorist groups would have greater difficulty obtaining the funds, weapons, materials, and secure areas they require to plan and conduct operations. More worrisome is that some of these countries also have the capability to manufacture weapons of mass destruction (WMD) that could get into the hands of terrorists. The United States will continue to insist that these countries end the support they give to terrorist groups.[112]

State has historically reported on states' WMD development and proliferation activities, even without direct evidence that the governments in question were proliferating that technology to terrorists. In 2002, it cited North Korea's sales of missile technology to Libya and Syria;[113] the following year, it praised Libya for agreeing to give up its WMD programs.[114] In 2005, it cited Iran's ability to produce chemical and biological weapons, speculating that Iran "could support terrorist organizations seeking to acquire WMD."[115] The U.S. Government also believes that North Korea possesses, or is developing, nuclear, chemical, and biological weapons (*supra* Sections III.G; *infra* Sections V.A & V.B).

---

112   U.S. Department of State, *Country Reports on Terrorism 2007*, 171.

113   U.S. Department of State, *Patterns of Global Terrorism: 2002*, 81.

114   U.S. Department of State, *Patterns of Global Terrorism: 2003*, 86, 91.

115   U.S. Department of State, *Country Reports on Terrorism 2005*, 173.

The Obama Administration has continued to cite WMD proliferation concerns as part of its annual reporting on terrorism. Its 2013 report said, "Iran remains a state of proliferation concern," cited Iran's failure to "suspend its sensitive nuclear proliferation activities," and accused Iran of violating "its international obligations regarding its nuclear program."[116] The report also cited Syria's "proliferation-sensitive materials and facilities, including Syria's significant stockpile of chemical weapons," speculating that those weapons "could find their way to terrorist organizations."[117]

By 2007, the Bush Administration had concluded that North Korea had provided substantial assistance with the construction of a reactor in Syria for the development of nuclear weapons (*infra* Section III.L). More recently, evidence published by a UN POE has proven that North Korea had assisted Syria with its chemical weapons program (*infra* Section V.B).

In recent years, the U.S. State Department has also cited diplomatic and military relations between SSOT-listed governments in its "Country Reports" descriptions of the state sponsorship of terrorism. For example, the 2005 "Country Reports" cited Cuba for its "friendly ties with Iran and North Korea" and for holding military talks with North Korea "at the general staff level ... in Pyongyang."[118] It also cited a visit by the North Korean Trade Minister to Havana, and the two nations' signing of "a protocol for cooperation in the areas of science and trade."[119]

The U.S. State Department has also consistently cited Syria's strong diplomatic and defense ties to Iran, including visits by Iran's President, Defense Minister, and National Security Advisor to Damascus (2007,[120] 2009,[121] and 2010[122]); a visit by Syria's President and Defense Minister to

---

116   U.S. Department of State, *Country Reports on Terrorism 2013*, 230.

117   *Id.* at 232.

118   U.S. Department of State, *Country Reports on Terrorism 2005*, 172.

119   *Id.*

120   U.S. Department of State, *Country Reports on Terrorism 2007*, 175.

121   U.S. Department of State, *Country Reports on Terrorism 2009* 195.

122   U.S. Department of State, *Country Reports on Terrorism 2010*, 153.

Tehran (2008,[123] 2009,[124] and 2010[125]); defense cooperation agreements between Iran and Syria (2008[126] and 2009[127]); and Syria's defense of Iran's policies and its nuclear ambitions (2008,[128] 2009,[129] 2010,[130] and 2011[131]). North Korea maintains close defense and scientific relationships with both countries (*infra* Sections III.G, III.L, IV.A & V.B).

The U.S. State Department reports have also cited Iran, Sudan, Syria, and North Korea (the latter as recently as 2012, more than three years after its removal from the SSOT list)[132] for their deficient regulatory regimes to combat the financing of terrorism, conduct that is passive, rather than the active sponsorship of terrorism (*infra* Section V.E).

8. Recency of Support for Terrorism

There is no legal time limit on what conduct may be a basis for an SSOT listing. The text of the Export Administration Act provides for no such limit, and its use of the term "repeatedly" implies that past conduct may be considered. Many of the U.S. State Department's prior SSOT justifications have cited conduct occurring years before a listing. For example, when the U.S. State Department added Sudan to the SSOT list in 1993, it found "no conclusive evidence linking the Government of Sudan to any specific terrorist incident during the year."[133] The U.S. State Department's 2000 annual terrorism report noted the U.S. government's "long memory" and commitment to holding terrorists accountable for past attacks "regardless of when the acts occurred."[134]

---

123   U.S. Department of State, *Country Reports on Terrorism 2008,* 185.

124   U.S. Department of State, *Country Reports on Terrorism 2009,* 195.

125   U.S. Department of State, *Country Reports on Terrorism 2010,* 153.

126   U.S. Department of State, *Country Reports on Terrorism 2008,* 185.

127   U.S. Department of State, *Country Reports on Terrorism 2009,* 195.

128   U.S. Department of State, *Country Reports on Terrorism 2008,* 185.

129   U.S. Department of State, *Country Reports on Terrorism 2007,* 175.

130   U.S. Department of State, *Country Reports on Terrorism 2007,* 175.

131   U.S. Department of State, *Country Reports on Terrorism 2007,* 175.

132   U.S. Department of State, *Country Reports on Terrorism 2007,* 175.

133   U.S. Department of State, *Country Reports on Terrorism 1993,* 25.

134   U.S. Department of State, Office of the Coordinator for Counterterrorism, "Overview of State-Sponsored Terrorism," in *Patterns of Global Terrorism: 2000.*

F. Legal Consequences of a SSOT Listing

1. Mandatory Financial Sanctions

A SSOT listing carries some important legal consequences for the targeted government. The most immediate of these is triggered by 18 U.S.C. § 2332d, a provision of the Criminal Code that prohibits financial transactions by U.S. persons with the governments of SSOT listed states, except in accordance with Treasury Department regulations, which are published at 31 C.F.R. Part 596, and which require that any such transactions by U.S. persons be licensed through the Treasury Department's Office of Foreign Assets Control.

Importantly, the definition of "U.S. person" also extends to U.S. financial institutions that process and clear international financial transactions denominated in U.S. dollars. Because more than 60% of the world's currency reserves are denominated in U.S. dollars,[135] this sanction, by itself, could constrain North Korea's access to the global financial system and close one important loophole in current U.S. sanctions against North Korea.[136]

2. Loss of Immunity from Tort Lawsuits for Terrorism or Torture

A second impact of a SSOT designation is that the targeted government loses its sovereign immunity from suits for personal injury or wrongful death due to the listed state's acts of terrorism or torture. The congressional report accompanying the 1995 passage of the terrorism exception to the Foreign Sovereign Immunities Act[137] specifically found that North Korea and other states considered terrorism "a legitimate instrument of achieving their foreign policy goals."[138]

---

135   International Monetary Fund, "Appendix Table I.2" in *Annual Report 2014: From Stabilization to Sustainable Growth* (July 2014), http://www.imf.org/external/pubs/ft/ar/2014/eng/.

136   To understand the importance of Part 596 sanctions, one must first understand that, contrary to the commonly expressed view, U.S. sanctions against North Korea are still among the weakest sanctions applicable to any sanctioned government. *See* Joshua Stanton, "North Korea: The Myth of Maxed-Out Sanctions," *Fletcher Security Review* 2.1 (21 January 2015).

137   28 U.S.C. § 1605A.

138   U.S. House Committee on the Judiciary. *Comprehensive Antiterrorism Act of 1995: report (to Accompany H.R. 1710).* (104 H. Rpt. 383).

The loss of immunity applies to only acts occurring while the state is designated as a SSOT, or which are reasons for the state's designation as a SSOT. As a result of judgments entered in the last five years, North Korea is already subject to over $400 million in adjudged liability for its torture or sponsorship of terrorist acts prior to October 11, 2008, the date of its SSOT list removal. North Korea has not entered an appearance in any U.S. court to defend against these suits.

In 2008, for example, several survivors of the U.S.S. *Pueblo* incident and the widow of the ship's commanding officer, Lloyd Bucher, won a $69 million judgment against the North Korean government.[139] A second suit alleged that North Korea provided training, weapons, money, and operational support to the Japanese Red Army and the Popular Front for the Liberation of Palestine, which carried out the 1972 Lod Airport Massacre. In 2010, a U.S. District Court ruled in favor of the plaintiffs and awarded them $378 million in compensatory and punitive damages.[140]

Other suits against North Korea are pending in U.S. federal courts. In July 2014, U.S. District Judge Royce Lamberth ruled that North Korea was liable for sponsoring rocket attacks by Hezbollah (*infra* Section III.J).[141] A federal appeals court recently remanded a fourth suit, by the surviving relatives of the Rev. Kim Dong-shik, whom North Korean agents allegedly kidnapped in China and murdered in North Korea, to the U.S. District Court for the District of Columbia, for entry of a default judgment against North Korea (*infra* Section III.I).[142]

3. U.S. Opposition to Benefits from International Financial Institutions

Finally, a SSOT designation requires U.S. representatives to oppose any benefits or extensions of credit to the listed states by international financial institutions, including loans from the World Bank and International Monetary Fund (22 U.S.C. § 2371),[143] and other international financial institutions, including the Asian Development Bank (22 U.S.C. § 262p-4q).[144] A separate provision[145]

---

139   *Massie v. Gov't of the Democratic People's Republic of Korea*, 592 F. Supp. 2d 57 (D.D.C. 2008).

140   *Calderon-Cardona v. Democratic People's Republic of Korea*, 723 F. Supp. 2d 441 (D.P.R. 2010).

141   *Kaplan v. Cent. Bank of the Islamic Republic of Iran*, Civil Action No. 10-483 (RCL) (D.D.C. July 23, 2014).

142   *Kim v. Democratic People's Republic of Korea*, No. 13-7147 (D.C. Cir. Dec. 23, 2014).

143   Foreign Assistance Act of 1961, Pub. L. No. 87-195, § 620A added by Pub. L. No. 94-329, § 303, 90 Stat. 753 (as amended).

144   Act of Oct. 3, 1977, Pub. L. No. 95-118, § 1621 added by Pub. L. No. 104-132, § 327, 110 Stat. 1257.

145   Because of North Korea's harboring of the four Japanese Red Army Hijackers, this provision would still apply to North Korea, notwithstanding its removal from the SSOT list.

requires U.S. representatives to use the "voice and vote" of the United States to channel assistance toward countries "that do not provide refuge to individuals committing acts of international terrorism by hijacking aircraft."[146]

4. OTHER EFFECTS

Other effects of a SSOT designation would be of little consequence,[147] either because of North Korea's self-imposed isolation, or because those effects would be redundant to additional restrictions already in effect. These include the denial of non-immigrant visas to nationals of terror-sponsoring states (8 U.S.C. § 1735);[148] prohibitions against the exports of munitions, luxury goods, or sensitive technology (15 C.F.R. § 746.2); and ineligibility for foreign assistance grants and loans (22 U.S.C. § 2377;[149] cf. id. §§ 2151n,[150] 2304[151]).

Similarly, North Korea is already ineligible for loans from the Export-Import Bank (12 U.S.C. § 635) because it is considered a "Marxist-Leninist" country.[152] Goods imported to the United States from SSOT-listed countries are ineligible for duty-free treatment, but for strictly economic reasons, and because of sanctions imposed by President Obama in 2011,[153] few North Korean products are imported into the United States. Companies and individuals are also denied tax credits for income earned in SSOT-listed countries. Companies in which a SSOT-listed government owns or controls a significant interest are ineligible for government contracts. It is unlikely that any of these latter sanctions would have a significant impact on North Korea.

---

146   Act of Oct. 3, 1977, Pub. L. No. 95-118, § 701(a), 91 Stat. 1069 (as amended).

147   U.S. Department of State, *Country Reports on Terrorism 2008*, 181-82.

148   Enhanced Border Security and Visa Entry Reform Act of 2002, Pub. L. No. 107-173, § 306, 116 Stat. 555.

149   Foreign Assistance Act of 1961, Pub. L. No. 87-195, § 620G added by Pub. L. No. 104-132, § 325, 110 Stat. 1256.

150   *Id.* at § 116 added by Pub. L. No. 94-161, § 310, 89 Stat. 860 (as amended).

151   *Id.* at § 502B added by Pub. L. No. 93-559, § 46, 88 Stat. 1815 (as amended).

152   Export-Import Bank Act of 1945, ch. 341, § 2(b)(2) added by Pub. L. No. 90-267, § 1(c), 82 Stat. 48 (as amended).

153   Exec. Order 13,570, 76 Fed. Reg. 22289 (Apr. 20, 2011).

G. Removal from the SSOT List

Section 6(j) of the Export Administration Act provides two parallel paths for the removal of a government from the SSOT list (formally known as "rescission").

One path, at Section 6(j)(4)(A), authorizes the President to certify to Congress[154] that "there has been a fundamental change in the leadership and policies of the government of the country concerned," that the listed government "is not supporting acts of international terrorism," and that it has "provided assurances that it will not support acts of international terrorism in the future."[155]

Under a second path, at Section 6(j)(4)(B), at least 45 days before a government is removed from the SSOT list, the President may certify to Congress that the listed government "has not provided any support for international terrorism during the preceding 6-month period," and "has provided assurances that it will not support acts of international terrorism in the future."[156] It was the second of these paths that President George W. Bush chose in removing North Korea from the SSOT list in October 2008 (*infra* Section III.M).

III. Before 2008: North Korea's Designation as a State Sponsor of Terrorism

Sections III through V of this report describe conduct that has justified, would justify, or could potentially justify North Korea's SSOT listing. They are not a complete list of North Korea's acts of terrorism or sponsorship of terrorism.

A. 1970–2015: Support for the Japanese Red Army

The origins of North Korea's placement on the SSOT list can be traced to 1970, when nine members of the Japanese Red Army hijacked a Japanese airliner to North Korea. Pyongyang has harbored the surviving hijackers ever since. Four of them are still living in North Korea today.[157]

---

154   Specifically, the Speaker of the House of Representatives; the Chairman of the Senate Committee on Banking, Housing, and Urban Affairs; and the Chairman of the Senate Foreign Relations Committee.

155   Export Administration Act of 1979, Pub. L. No. 96-72, § 6(j)(4)(A) added by Pub. L. No. 101-222, § 4, 103 Stat. 1897.

156   *Id.* at § 6(j)(4)(B) added by Pub. L. No. 101-222, § 4, 103 Stat. 1897.

157   "1970 Hijackers living in North Korea to start posting on Twitter," *The Japan Times*, 01 October 2014.

Although North Korea's harboring of the hijackers has been cited in the U.S. State Department's annual reports from the 1980s until the present day,[158] the Japanese Red Army was not designated as a Foreign Terrorist Organization before October 1997, and was designated as such only until October 2001.[159]

The U.S. State Department's annual reports on terrorism have not cited North Korea's sponsorship of a far deadlier attack by the Japanese Red Army—the 1972 massacre at Lod Airport, Israel. The attack killed 26 people, including 17 Americans, and injured 79 others. The American victims were religious pilgrims from Puerto Rico. Two terrorists also died in the attack. On July 16, 2010, a U.S. District Court held that North Korea had provided the Japanese Red Army with training, weapons, financial assistance, and other operational assistance in support of the attack. The court ordered North Korea to pay $378 million in compensatory and punitive damages to the plaintiffs.[160]

B. 1979–1986: SMALL-SCALE SUPPORT FOR FTOs, THE RANGOON BOMBING

North Korea's first prominent mention in the U.S. State Department's annual "Patterns of Global Terrorism" followed a 1983 bombing in Rangoon by North Korean agents, in an attempt to assassinate South Korean President Chun Doo-hwan. The bombing killed 21 people.[161] In its 1983 annual report, the U.S. State Department called the 1983 Rangoon bombing "[t]he most vicious terrorist attack in Asia in 1983."[162] The U.S. State Department did not designate North Korea as a SSOT following this attack, but in subsequent years, the U.S. State Department would sometimes cite the 1983 bombing as one of the acts that contributed to North Korea's SSOT listing.[163]

In 1984, the U.S. State Department reported that "P'yongyang almost certainly continues to provide training, funds, and weapons to various foreign extremist groups." It voiced suspicions that

---

158   U.S. Department of State, *Patterns of Global Terrorism: 1988*, 48-49.

159   U.S. Department of State, "Foreign Terrorist Organizations," http://www.state.gov/j/ct/rls/other/des/123085.htm.

160   *Calderon-Cardona v. Democratic People's Republic of Korea*, 723 F. Supp. 2d 441 (D.P.R. 2010).

161   A declassified CIA report on the bombing is available at http://www.foia.cia.gov/sites/default/files/document_conversions/89801/DOC_0000408056.pdf.

162   U.S. Department of State, *Patterns of Global Terrorism: 1983*, 19.

163   U.S. Department of State, *Patterns of Global Terrorism: 1989*, 47.

North Korea sold "large quantities of ordnance to Iran," but conceded that "[t]here is no evidence to date ... that these weapons are acquired and used by those who engage in terrorism."[164]

In 1985, the U.S. State Department asserted that North Korea "almost certainly has continued to provide training, funds, and weapons to various foreign extremist groups."[165] In 1986, the U.S. State Department noted that "South Korea blamed North Korea for the bombing of Seoul's Kimpo Airport on the eve of the Asian Games in September 1986, but no evidence has been found that clearly links the attack to P'yongyang."[166]

C. 1987: THE KAL 858 BOMBING AND NORTH KOREA'S SSOT LISTING

On November 29, 1987, North Korean agents placed a bomb aboard Korean Air Flight 858, from Abu Dhabi to Bangkok. The bomb exploded over the Andaman Sea and killed all 115 people aboard the flight. The U.S. State Department's 1987 annual report called the bombing that year's "single most lethal international terrorist attack." North Korea was implicated when the bombers were arrested:

> A couple who boarded the flight in Baghdad and left it in Abu Dhabi were arrested in Bahrain on 1 December for traveling on false Japanese passports as father and daughter. As they were being interrogated, they bit into cyanide capsules concealed in cigarettes. The man died, but the woman survived and was later deported to Seoul. She has since publicly confirmed that the pair were North Korean intelligence agents who had placed the bomb on the aircraft in their carry-on luggage.

> According to the surviving terrorist, the KA 858 bombing was the start of a campaign to disrupt the Olympic Games in 1988. We believe it possible that the bombing was the first in a planned series of terrorist events intended to portray South Korea as unsafe. North

---

164   U.S. Department of State, Office of the Ambassador-at-Large for Counter-Terrorism, *Patterns of Global Terrorism: 1984* (November 1985), http://www.higginsctc.org/patternsofglobalterrorism/1984PoGT.pdf, 21.

165   U.S. Department of State, Office of the Ambassador-at-Large for Counter-Terrorism, *Patterns of Global Terrorism: 1985* (October 1986), 8.

166   U.S. Department of State, Office of the Ambassador-at-Large for Counter-Terrorism, *Patterns of Global Terrorism: 1986* (January 1988), 11.

Korea will probably not host any Olympic events in P'yongyang or participate in the Games—a situation that might encourage it to stage further disruptive acts.

The report states that the bombing of Flight 858 "heralded the return of North Korea as an active agent of state terrorism for the first time since it bombed the Martyr's Memorial in Rangoon four years earlier."[167]

On January 20, 1988, Secretary of State George P. Schultz designated North Korea as a SSOT because of the bombing.[168] The U.S. State Department's 1989 report confirmed that "North Korea remains on the list of state sponsors of terrorism "because of its responsibility for the November 1987 destruction of a South Korean airliner and the 1983 terrorist attack against Republic of Korea officials in Rangoon, Burma."[169] In its 1990 report,[170] the U.S. State Department cited the testimony of captured North Korea agent Kim Hyun-Hui, who alleged that Kim Jong-Il had personally ordered the bombing of Flight 858.[171]

D. 1990–1999: Continued Support for Terrorist Groups; Assassination of South Korean Official

In its 1990 annual report, the U.S. State Department accused North Korea of supporting the New Peoples' Army,[172] a Communist insurgent group in the Philippines that would be designated as a Foreign Terrorist Organization in 2002.[173]

---

167   U.S. Department of State, Office of the Ambassador-at-Large for Counter-Terrorism, *Patterns of Global Terrorism: 1987* (August 1988), http://www.higginsctc.org/patternsofglobalterrorism/1987pogt.pdf, 39.

168   "Certification of Rescission of North Korea's Designation as a State Sponsor of Terrorism: Memorandum for the Secretary of State," 73 Fed. Reg. 37351 (July 1, 2008).

169   U.S. Department of State, *Patterns of Global Terrorism: 1989*, 47.

170   U.S. Department of State, *Patterns of Global Terrorism: 1990*, 7.

171   As recently as 2007, State's annual "Country Reports" stated that South Korea was "[t]raditionally focused on potential *terrorism* from" North Korea (emphasis added, *Country Reports on Terrorism 2007*, 28). North Korea is not known to have directed or sponsored any attacks against South Korea by non-state actors.

172   U.S. Department of State, *Patterns of Global Terrorism: 1990*, 33.

173   U.S. Department of State, "Foreign Terrorist Organizations," http://www.state.gov/j/ct/rls/other/des/123085.htm.

As early as its 1992 annual report, however, the U.S. State Department began to soften its descriptions of North Korea's sponsorship of terrorism. That year was significant for the debut of an early version of the U.S. State Department doctrine that survives to this day: "The Democratic People's Republic of Korea (DPRK or North Korea) is not known to have sponsored any terrorist acts since 1987, when a KAL airliner was bombed in flight." Although the report noted North Korea's "ambiguous condemnation of international terrorism," it credited it for "honoring its pledge to abandon violence against South Korea" and "suspend[ing] its support for the Communist New People's Army" in the Philippines.[174]

The 1992 report also mentioned "a Korean resident of Japan allegedly kidnapped by North Koreans to teach Japanese to DPRK terrorists involved in the 1987 KAL bombing," foreshadowing the wider issue of North Korean abductions of Japanese citizens.[175]

Throughout the 1990s, U.S. State Department reports remained mostly consistent with this form, with minor variations. The 1996 report also took note of South Korean suspicions that "North Korean agents were involved in the murder of a South Korean official in Vladivostok on 1 October 1996."[176]

The 1996 report also raised an issue that would emerge as a larger controversy between the United States and North Korea[177]—the arrest of Red Army Faction member Yoshimi Tanaka in Cambodia for carrying counterfeit $100 bills.[178] That revelation added to a growing body of evidence that North Korea was counterfeiting U.S. currency, and also linked North Korea's sponsorship of terrorism to its counterfeiting operations.

174   U.S. Department of State, Office of the Coordinator for Counterterrorism, *Patterns of Global Terrorism: 1992* (April 1993), http://www.higginsctc.org/patternsofglobalterrorism/1992POGT.pdf, 24.

175   *Id.*

176   U.S. Department of State, "Overview of State-Sponsored Terrorism: North Korea," in *Patterns of Global Terrorism: 1996.*

177   *Id.*

178   Nicholas D. Kristof, "Is North Korea Turning to Counterfeiting?," *The New York Times*, 17 April 1996.

E. 1997–2004: Terrorist Financing

On September 30, 2004, a grand jury of the U.S. District Court for the District of Columbia indicted Sean Garland, the Chief of Staff of the Real Irish Republican Army (IRA),[179] a Marxist IRA splinter group that the U.S. State Department had designated as a Foreign Terrorist Organization on May 16, 2001.[180] The charges included conspiracy, dealing in counterfeit obligations or securities, and counterfeit acts committed outside the United States.[181] Garland was not indicted for providing material support to a terrorist organization.[182]

According to the indictment, starting in 1997 or earlier, and until as recently as 2004, Garland and several co-conspirators smuggled high-quality counterfeit U.S. currency made in North Korea, commonly known as "supernotes," into Ireland and the United Kingdom.[183] Garland and his associates obtained the supernotes from North Korean embassies in third countries, and laundered them for a profit. The indictment quotes two of Garland's co-conspirators as telling a third person that the proceeds of the sale "all go[es] back into the organization."

According to the indictment, the detection of supernotes briefly caused both Irish and Thai banks to cease accepting $100 notes. The U.S. Government asked the Irish Government to extradite Mr. Garland for trial in the United States, but in January 2012, a Justice of the High Court of Ireland denied the request.[184] The U.S. Government did not appeal the decision.

---

179   Also known as the Official IRA, or the Red IRA.

180   U.S. Department of State, "Foreign Terrorist Organizations," http://www.state.gov/j/ct/rls/other/des/123085.htm.

181   Grand Jury Indictment, *United States v. Garland*, Case No. 1:05-cr-00185 (RMC) (D.D.C. May 19, 2005).

182   For more background information on North Korea's counterfeiting of U.S. currency, *see* Stephen Mihm, "No Ordinary Counterfeit," *The New York Times,* 23 July 2006; David Rose, "North Korea's Dollar Store," September 2009, *Vanity Fair*; Raphael F. Perl and Dick K. Nanto, "North Korean Counterfeiting of U.S. Currency," *CRS Report for Congress RL33324* (17 January 2007); and Raphael F. Perl, "Drug Trafficking and North Korea: Issues for U.S. Policy," *CRS Report for Congress RL32167* (25 January 2007). In 2008, a federal court in Las Vegas convicted Chen Chiang Liu of conspiring to smuggle supernotes into the United States (Adrienne Packer, "Conviction in counterfeit currency case," *Las Vegas Review-Journal*, 18 September 2008). In April 2013, David Cohen, the Undersecretary of the Treasury for Terrorism and Financial Intelligence, said, "We believe North Korea is continuing to try to pass a supernote into the international financial system" ("U.S. Pursuing North Korean Leader's Secret Money, Official Says," *Voice of America*, 13 April 2013).

183   Grand Jury Indictment, *United States v. Garland*, Case No. 1:05-cr-00185 (RMC), 17 (D.D.C. May 19, 2005).

184   "Sean Garland will not be extradited to US," *RTE News,* 07 March 2012.

F. 1999–2001: STATE TESTS THE WATERS FOR DE-LISTING

In its 1999 annual report, the U.S. State Department first hinted at removing North Korea from the SSOT list:

> There have been some encouraging signs recently suggesting that some countries are considering taking steps to distance themselves from terrorism. North Korea has made some positive statements condemning terrorism in all its forms. We have outlined clearly to the Government of North Korea the steps it must take to be removed from the list, all of which are consistent with its stated policies.[185]

The report stated that "if a state sponsor meets the criteria for being dropped from the terrorism list, it will be removed—notwithstanding other differences we may have with a country's other policies and actions."[186]

According to a 2008 Congressional Research Service report, North Korea demanded in 2000 that it be removed from the SSOT list.[187] The U.S. State Department's 2000 annual report, however, was much less encouraging, noting the U.S. Government's "long memory" and commitment to holding terrorists accountable for past attacks.[188] The report noted that, in talks with U.S. diplomats, North Korea had "reiterated its opposition to terrorism and agreed to support international actions against such activity."[189] As justification for North Korea's continued listing, however, the report noted North Korea's continued harboring of the Japanese Red Army hijackers and suspected weapons sales to terrorists,[190] including the Moro Islamic Liberation Front in the Philippines.[191]

---

185   U.S. Department of State, *Patterns of Global Terrorism: 1999*, 3.

186   *Id.* at 2.

187   Larry Niksch, "North Korea: Terrorism List Removal?," *CRS Report for Congress RL30613* (06 November 2008), http://fpc.state.gov/documents/organization/112015.pdf, 3.

188   U.S. Department of State, "Overview of State-Sponsored Terrorism," in *Patterns of Global Terrorism: 2000.*

189   *Id.*

190   *Id.*

191   The Moro Islamic Liberation Front is not designated as a Foreign Terrorist Organization.

The U.S. State Department's 2001 annual report, the first report following the September 11, 2001 attacks, was more critical, calling North Korea's response to international efforts to combat terrorism "disappointing," despite North Korea's post-9/11 statement expressing its opposition to terrorism, its signature of the UN Convention for the Suppression of the Financing of Terrorism, and its accession to the Convention Against the Taking of Hostages. It criticized North Korea for failing to provide information on its implementation of UN Security Council resolutions intended to combat terrorism, including the blocking of terrorist assets.[192]

As in previous reports, the U.S. State Department cited North Korea's continued harboring of Japanese Red Army hijackers, and also cited "some evidence" that North Korea had sold "limited quantities" of small arms to terrorists during the previous year. Significantly, it also raised the issue of North Korea's nuclear weapons programs and its failure to progress toward implementing the 1994 Agreed Framework.[193]

G. WMD PROLIFERATION

North Korea began construction of its 5-megawatt reactor at Yongbyon in 1979.[194] The reactor became operational in 1986. By the late 1980s, the U.S. Government became concerned that North Korea would use the reactor to produce plutonium for nuclear weapons. In 1994, the United States and North Korea signed an Agreed Framework in which the United States agreed to provide North Korea energy assistance and food aid in exchange for North Korea's dismantling of its nuclear programs. The agreement collapsed in 2002 after North Korea admitted to, and then subsequently denied, having a secret uranium enrichment program.

North Korea has long been suspected of having chemical and biological weapons programs.[195] In 2004, the British Broadcasting Corporation aired a documentary, "Access to Evil," in which a former guard at Camp 22 alleged that he witnessed the death of a family of four during a test of chemical weapons in an experimental gas chamber.[196]

---

192   U.S. Department of State, *Patterns of Global Terrorism: 2001*, 68.

193   *Id.*

194   "Yongbyon 5MWe Reactor," *Nuclear Threat Initiative*, last modified 19 March 2014, http://www.nti.org/facilities/766/.

195   In 1998, the author of this report, while serving as an officer in U.S. Forces Korea, was required to receive a series of anthrax inoculation injections.

196   "Access to Evil," *BBC News*, 29 January 2004, http://news.bbc.co.uk/2/hi/programmes/this_world/3436701.stm.

In the years after the September 11, 2001 attacks, North Korea's nuclear program and its potential proliferation to terrorists (or other sponsors of terrorism) became an additional basis for North Korea's SSOT listing. The U.S. State Department's 2002 terrorism report, for example, cited North Korea's sale of missile technology to other state sponsors of terrorism.[197] Its 2005 terrorism report cited Pyongyang's "capability to manufacture WMD and other destabilizing technologies that can get into the hands of terrorists" and noted that North Korea "continued to maintain … ties to terrorist groups."[198]

North Korea has long provided ballistic missile technology to Syria and Iran,[199] and for many years, had a nuclear weapons development partnership with Pakistan.[200] One *New York Times* report from 2004 described an intense controversy within the U.S. intelligence community as to whether that partnership included a joint nuclear test between North Korea and Pakistan in 1998.[201]

In 2005, *The Washington Post* reported that Department of Energy experts had concluded that North Korea had exported uranium hexafluoride to Libya. The experts had analyzed the low-enriched uranium after Libya surrendered its nuclear weapons program that year.[202]

North Korea has an extensive history of nuclear cooperation with Syria.[203] That relationship eventually conceived the Al-Kibar nuclear reactor,[204] which the Israeli Air Force destroyed in

197   U.S. Department of State, *Patterns of Global Terrorism: 2002*, 81.

198   U.S. Department of State, *Country Reports on Terrorism 2005*, 171.

199   Paul K. Kerr, Mary Beth D. Nikitin and Steven A. Hildreth, "Iran-North Korea-Syria Ballistic Missile and Nuclear Cooperation," *CRS Report for Congress R43480* (16 April 2014), http://fpc.state.gov/documents/organization/225867.pdf.

200   Sharon A. Squassoni, "Weapons of Mass Destruction: Trade Between North Korea and Pakistan," *CRS Report for Congress RL31900* (11 October 2006), http://fas.org/spp/starwars/crs/RL31900.pdf.

201   David E. Sanger and William J. Broad, "Pakistan May Have Aided North Korea A-Test," *The New York Times*, 27 February 2004.

202   Glenn Kessler, "North Korea May Have Sent Libya Nuclear Material, U.S. Tells Allies," *The Washington Post*, 02 February 2005.

203   Anthony H. Cordesman, "Syrian Weapons of Mass Destruction: An Overview," *Center for Strategic and International Studies* (02 June 2008), http://csis.org/files/media/csis/pubs/080602_syrianwmd.pdf.

204   Mario Profaca, "CIA video showing suspected Syrian nuclear reactor," *YouTube* video, 6:03, 25 April 2008, https://www.youtube.com/watch?v=yj62GRd0Te8.

2007 (*infra* Section III.L).[205] Suspicions of North Korean nuclear cooperation with Iran[206] are more controversial.[207]

North Korea has threatened to provide nuclear weapons to terrorists. On April 23, 2005, retired *Washington Post* reporter Selig Harrison, who frequently carried messages from the North Korean government to Washington, told *Kyodo News* that North Korean officials in Pyongyang had told him, "The United States should consider the danger that we could transfer nuclear weapons to terrorists, that we have the ability to do so."[208]

Eventually, as explained in Sections III.K and III.M, the prospect of a diplomatic dismantling of North Korea's nuclear program would become the Bush Administration's overriding basis for removing North Korea from the SSOT list.

H. 2002–2008: Revelation of Abductions of Japanese Citizens

In 2002, North Korea admitted to long-standing suspicions that in the 1970s and 1980s, its agents, possibly agents of the RGB (*supra* Section II.E.6), had abducted an unknown number of Japanese citizens, most of them from Japanese soil.[209] The abductions, and their relationship to North Korea's SSOT listing, would become an important issue in U.S.-Japanese relations.[210] They continue to complicate[211] U.S.-Japanese coordination of North Korea policy to this day.[212]

---

205   A January 2015 news story published in *Der Spiegel* alleges that North Korea, Iran, and Hezbollah are jointly assisting Syria with an ongoing nuclear weapons program (Erich Follath, "Assad's Secret: Evidence Points to Syrian Push for Nuclear Weapons," *Der Spiegel*, 09 January 2015).

206   Larry Niksch, "North Korea: Terrorism List Removal?," *CRS Report for Congress RL30613* (06 November 2008), 28-31.

207   Paul K. Kerr, Mary Beth D. Nikitin and Steven A. Hildreth, "Iran-North Korea-Syria Ballistic Missile and Nuclear Cooperation," *CRS Report for Congress R43480* (16 April 2014).

208   Sonni Efron, "U.S. Looks to China to Rein In North Korea," *Los Angeles Times*, 23 April 2005.

209   Yoshi Yamamoto, *Taken!* (Washington, D.C.: Committee for Human Rights in North Korea, 2011).

210   Emma Chanlett-Avery, "North Korea's Abduction of Japanese Citizens and the Six-Party Talks," *CRS Report for Congress RS22845* (19 March 2008), https://www.fas.org/sgp/crs/row/RS22845.pdf.

211   Atsushi Okudera, "U.S. fears eased sanctions will embolden North Korea," *The Asahi Shimbun*, 05 July 2014.

212   "U.S. warns Abe against visiting North Korea," *The Japan Times*, 16 July 2014.

A 2008 Congressional Research Service report, citing a Japanese organization advocating on the abductees' behalf, alleges that in 2001, the Bush Administration assured the Japanese government "that the United States would continue to raise the kidnapping issue with North Korea and would not remove North Korea from the U.S. list of terrorism-supporting countries."[213]

Despite the revelations, North Korea persisted in its demand that it be removed from the SSOT list.[214] The U.S. State Department's annual terrorism reports have mentioned North Korea's failure to account for all of the abductees ever since, and until 2008, the U.S. State Department had cited this failure as a reason for North Korea's SSOT listing.[215]

In Japan, political pressure grew for Prime Minister Junichiro Koizumi to obtain the abductees' release. In 2002, secret negotiations between Japan and North Korea resulted in the return of five abductees and six of their children. As Koizumi continued to negotiate for the return of other abductees, the Bush Administration pressed the Japanese government not to provide North Korea with financial aid in exchange for the return of the abductees until North Korea complied with its disarmament obligations.[216]

Talks between Japan and North Korea broke down soon thereafter, and top Bush Administration officials publicly assured Japan that North Korea would not be removed from the SSOT list before the abductees—or their remains—were returned to Japan:

> In April 2004, the State Department emphasized the kidnapping of Japanese citizens in its justification for North Korean's inclusion on the U.S. list of terrorism-supporting countries, as part of the Department's annual report on international terrorism. The State Department's Patterns of Global Terrorism 2003 described Kim Jong-il's admission of North Korean kidnapping during his meeting with Japanese Prime Minister Koizumi in September 2002 and that Japan-North Korea negotiations over the issue were continuing. Coffer Black, the State Department's top counterterrorism official, stated upon the release of the report that the kidnapping issue was

---

213   Larry Niksch, "North Korea: Terrorism List Removal?," *CRS Report for Congress RL30613* (06 November 2008), 6.

214   *Id.* at 3.

215   U.S. Department of State, *Country Reports on Terrorism 2007* (April 2008), 173.

216   Larry Niksch, "North Korea: Terrorism List Removal?," *CRS Report for Congress RL30613* (06 November 2008), 6-7.

Joshua Stanton

a key factor in the report's designation of North Korea as a state sponsor of terrorism. During this period, President Bush, Vice President Cheney, and National Security Adviser Condoleezza Rice made public statements pledging to support Japan. At his summit meeting with Prime Minister Koizumi in May 2003, President Bush stated: "Abduction is an abominable act. The United States supports Japan completely until we find out the whereabouts of each and every Japanese citizen who has been abducted by North Korea." Condoleezza Rice described the kidnapping issue as "a priority also for the United States, that we abhor what the North Koreans have done." In April 2004, Vice President Cheney said in Tokyo that Americans shared Japan's "outrage" over North Korea's kidnappings and that the Bush Administration supported Japan's demand for a "resolution of all the issues surrounding the criminal abduction of your citizens by the regime in Pyongyang."[217]

In April of 2006, President Bush met with Sakie Yokota, the mother of Megumi Yokota, who was abducted from Japan at the age of 13. President Bush described this as "one of the most moving meetings since I've been the President here in the Oval Office."[218]

The abduction revelations also increased congressional opposition to removing North Korea from the SSOT list. In 2005, the House of Representatives adopted a concurrent resolution condemning North Korea's abductions of Japanese and South Korean citizens, and one U.S. permanent resident, the Rev. Kim Dong-shik.[219]

I. 2005: ABDUCTION AND SUSPECTED MURDER OF REV. KIM DONG-SHIK

On January 28, 2005, the entire Illinois congressional delegation signed a letter to Pak Gil-yon, the North Korean Ambassador to the United Nations. The letter demanded that North Korea account for the fate of the Rev. Kim Dong-shik, whom the signers compared to Raoul Wallenberg and Harriet Tubman. Rev. Kim, a U.S. lawful permanent resident living in Illinois, disappeared in China in 2000, while assisting North Korean refugees. In 2004, the Seoul District Prosecutor's Office found that North Korean agents had kidnapped Rev. Kim from China and taken him to North Korea. The signatories to the letter stated as follows:

---

217   *Id.* at 6.

218   "President Meets with North Korean Defectors and Family Members of Abducted by North Korea," *The White House*, 28 April 2006, http://georgewbush-whitehouse.archives.gov/news/releases/2006/04/20060428-1.html.

219   H. Con. Res. 168, 109th Cong. (2005).

> We, therefore, wish to inform the Government of the Democratic People's Republic of Korea (DPRK) that we will NOT support the removal of your government from the State Department list of State Sponsors of Terrorism until such time, among other reasons, as a full accounting is provided to the Kim family regarding the fate of Reverend Kim Dong-shik following his abduction into North Korea five years ago.

The letter contains the signatures of some of America's most powerful politicians—House Speaker Dennis Hastert, House International Relations Committee Chairman Henry Hyde, Senator Dick Durbin, future Chicago Mayor Rahm Emanuel, and the Junior Senator from Illinois, Barack Obama.[220]

In the following years, press reports would reveal more details about Rev. Kim's abduction and death. A South Korean news story, citing South Korean intelligence sources, reported that one of the North Korea kidnappers admitted that he and his accomplices "grabbed Reverend Kim by the arm and pushed him into a taxi," and then "took away his cell phone and $1,000 in cash."[221] According to a 2008 *Washington Post* story, "The trial revealed that an abduction team spent 10 months plotting the seizure, grabbing Kim in front of a restaurant when he got into a taxi. The taxi took him to another car, which brought him to the border." Rev. Kim's widow[222] told *The Washington Post* that she had received reports that, following his abduction, her husband's health had deteriorated quickly.[223] Within a year, his weight fell from 180 pounds to 75 pounds. Shortly thereafter, Rev. Kim died and was buried in "a restricted area controlled by the North Korean Army."[224]

---

220   *See* http://freekorea.us/wp-content/uploads/2008/05/obama-letter.pdf.

221   "New suspect in North kidnapping," *Korea JoongAng Daily*, 14 January 2010.

222   A 2001 letter from Mrs. Kim is archived at http://web.archive.org/web/20011114091420/http://www.sowingseedsoffaith.com/Esther_Kim_Prayers.htm.

223   Glenn Kessler, "N. Korea's Abduction of U.S. Permanent Resident Fades From Official View," *The Washington Post,* 19 June 2008.

224   The U.S. State Department's 2002 *Country Reports on Human Rights Practices for North Korea*, however, references "unconfirmed reports that in January 2000 North Korean agents kidnaped [*sic*] a South Korean citizen, Reverend Kim Dong Shik, in China and took him to North Korea" (http://www.state.gov/j/drl/rls/hrrpt/2002/18249.htm).

None of the U.S. State Department's annual terrorism reports has ever mentioned Rev. Kim.[225] The omission was particularly conspicuous, given the strength of the evidence implicating North Korea in his disappearance. In December 2004, South Korean prosecutors named Yoo Young-hwa,[226] whom they described as "a Chinese-born ethnic Korean agent with North Korea's State Safety and Security Agency," as one of Rev. Kim's kidnappers.[227] In January 2005, Yoo pled guilty to Rev. Kim's kidnapping;[228] he was subsequently sentenced to a ten-year prison term.

In January 2010, South Korea's *Joongang Daily* reported that South Korea had arrested and was questioning a second suspect,[229] identified only as "Kim," in Rev. Kim's abduction.[230]

By 2007, however, the revelation of Rev. Kim's abduction and suspected murder was inconvenient to the U.S. State Department's policy objectives.[231] Beginning in 2006, senior U.S. State Department officials sought the authority to remove North Korea from the SSOT list in the course of their nuclear negotiations with Pyongyang. In February 2007, a U.S. diplomat signed a commitment to "begin the process" of removing North Korea from the SSOT list.[232]

---

225   Yoo's surname is sometimes rendered as "Ryu" when translated into English.

226   "Ethnic Korean 'Mole' Helped N.K. Spies Abduct Pastor in China," *The Chosun Ilbo*, 14 December 2004.

227   Kenneth Chan, "N. Korean Agent Confesses to Aiding in Abduction of S. Korean Pastor," *The Christian Post*, 31 January 2005.

228   "Seoul Court Sentences Man Who Helped North Korea Kidnap South Korean," *Voice of America*, 29 October 2009.

229   "New suspect in North kidnapping," *Korea JoongAng Daily*, 14 January 2010.

230   Presumably, no relation. Approximately 22% of ethnic Koreans have the surname Kim.

231   On at least one occasion, those involved in the negotiations with North Korea pressured another bureau in the U.S. State Department to change the content of its annual human rights country report on North Korea to avoid potential objections by the North Korean government. In 2008, *Washington Post* columnist Al Kamen reported that, according to leaked U.S. State Department e-mails, Glyn Davies, who would later become the U.S. State Department's Special Representative for North Korea Policy, asked his colleagues at the Bureau for Democracy, Human Rights, and Labor to "sacrifice a few adjectives for the cause" in the course of preparing its annual report on North Korea's human rights practices. The "cause" Davies referred to was "the Secretary's priority on the Six-Party Talks" (Al Kamen, "'Regime' Changed," *The Washington Post*, 05 March 2008). This suggests one possible explanation of the omission of Rev. Kim's case from the U.S. State Department's reports on terrorism.

232   Paul Kerr, "Initial Pact Reached to End North Korean Nuclear Weapons Program," *Arms Control Today*, 01 March 2007.

In 2008, Rev. Kim's widow told a *Washington Post* reporter that she had sent Assistant Secretary Christopher Hill a letter, pleading for him to raise her husband's case with the North Koreans.[233] In the *Post*'s story, Hill claimed to have "no memory" of receiving the letter; however, a former congressional staffer provided the author of this report a photograph of what he represents to be Hill receiving the letter directly from Congresswoman Ileana Ros-Lehtinen, then the Ranking Member of the House Foreign Affairs Committee.[234]

Having failed to obtain meaningful assistance from the political branches of her government, in 2009, Mrs. Kim sued the North Korean government for the abduction, torture, and murder of her husband in the U.S. District Court for the District of Columbia.[235] Mrs. Kim's suit was only possible because of an amendment to the Foreign Sovereign Immunities Act that allowed for suits against a foreign government, for damages arising from acts of terrorism and torture, committed while the government was listed as a state sponsor of terrorism (*supra* Section II.F.2).[236] A District Court dismissed the suit in 2013, finding that the plaintiffs had failed to plead direct evidence that Rev. Kim was tortured.[237] The District Court's decision, nonetheless, disclosed evidence that the U.S. State Department also believed that North Korea was behind Rev. Kim's kidnapping:

> A recently declassified internal State Department cable dated February 3, 2000, from representatives stationed in Seoul communicating with headquarters in Washington, D.C., states that a local Chinese paper reported that Chinese investigators had "strong evidence" that Reverend Kim was kidnapped from China by DPRK agents who had crossed over into China in late December to plan the abduction. Id. ¶ 26, Ex. G. The cable—authored a mere two weeks after Reverend Kim's abduction—further reported that ten people were involved in Reverend Kim's kidnapping, including a couple posing as North

---

233   Glenn Kessler, "N. Korea's Abduction of U.S. Permanent Resident Fades From Official View," *The Washington Post*, 19 June 2008.

234   *See* http://freekorea.us/wp-content/uploads/2008/06/img_0249.JPG.

235   First Amended Complaint, *Kim v. Democratic People's Republic of Korea*, Civil Action No. 09-648 (RWR) (D.D.C. Nov. 24, 2009).

236   28 U.S.C. § 1605A.

237   *Kim v. Democratic People's Republic of Korea*, 950 F. Supp. 2d 29 (D.D.C. 2013).

Korean defectors, and that Reverend Kim was held hostage in China before being transported into North Korea by his captors.[238]

In 2014, the U.S. Court of Appeals for the District of Columbia Circuit reversed the District Court's decision and remanded the case,[239] finding the evidence of North Korea's torture and murder of Rev. Kim sufficient to require a default judgment against North Korea, which failed to enter an appearance to contest the suit.[240] In its decision, the Court of Appeals acknowledged uncertainty about the evidence that North Korea tortured or murdered Rev. Kim, but cited the South Korean conviction and found that there was "no question that North Korean operatives abducted Reverend Kim in 2000 after the government found out about his activities."[241]

J. 2006-2014: REPORTS OF MATERIAL SUPPORT FOR HEZBOLLAH AND THE TAMIL TIGERS

In October 14, 2006, the UN Security Council approved Resolution 1718, which prohibited North Korea from exporting "any battle tanks, armoured combat vehicles, large calibre artillery systems, combat aircraft, attack helicopters, warships, missiles or missile systems."[242] It was the first of several increasingly stringent, but poorly enforced, resolutions that would eventually ban North Korea's weapons trade.

In 2006 and 2007, a series of stories by *Intelligence Online,* a French publication later cited in a 2008 Congressional Research Service report, alleged that North Korea had been training and arming Hezbollah since the 1980s. Among the Hezbollah leaders alleged to have received training in North Korea were "Hassan Nasrallah, Hezbollah's secretary-general and head of Hezbollah's military organization; Ibrahim Akil, the head of Hezbollah's security and intelligence service; and Mustapha Badreddine, Hezbollah's counter-espionage chief."[243]

---

238   *Id.* at 37.

239   Carol Morello, "U.S. court: North Korea liable for damages in kidnapping case," *The Washington Post*, 23 December 2014.

240   *Kim v. Democratic People's Republic of Korea*, No. 13-7147 (D.C. Cir. Dec. 23, 2014).

241   *Id.* at 3-4.

242   Security Council resolution 1718, para. 8, U.N. Doc. S/RES/1718 (14 October 2006) at http://www.un.org/Docs/journal/asp/ws.asp?m=s/res/1718%282006%29.

243   Larry Niksch, "North Korea: Terrorism List Removal?," *CRS Report for Congress RL30613* (06 November 2008), 20.

Intelligence Online reported that after 2000, North Korea also sent trainers to Hezbollah-controlled areas in Lebanon, and assisted Hezbollah with the construction of an extensive system of tunnels and underground bunkers. The Congressional Research Service report also cited consistent reports by Japan's conservative *Sankei Shimbun*, Britain's Arabic-language *Al-Sharq Al-Awsat*, and Lenny Ben-David, a former Israeli diplomat. According to the reports, the bunker system significantly improved Hezbollah's military capabilities during its 2006 war with Israel.[244]

The Congressional Research Service report also raised suspicions that North Korea was supplying longer-range artillery rockets to Hezbollah through Iran,[245] although these reports would not be confirmed for another year, after North Korea was removed from the SSOT list (*infra* Section IV.A).

A 2007 Congressional Research Service report also alleges that between 2006 and 2007, North Korea made "several ... attempts" to "smuggle conventional arms, including machine guns, automatic rifles, and anti-tank rocket launchers" to the Liberation Tigers of Tamil Eelam,[246] a group that was designated as a Foreign Terrorist Organization on October 8, 1997:[247]

> The Sri Lankan navy intercepted and attacked several North Korean ships carrying the arms. It sunk two of the vessels, captured several North Korean crewmen, and seized some of the North Korean arms. The Sri Lankan government filed an official protest with the North Korean government. U.S. intelligence agencies, using spy satellites, may have conveyed information about the North Korean ships to the Sri Lankan government, according to the reports.[248]

---

244 *Id.* at 20-21.

245 *Id.* at 22.

246 Larry Niksch and Raphael Perl, "North Korea: Terrorism List Removal?," *CRS Report for Congress RL30613* (11 December 2007), 18.

247 U.S. Department of State, "Foreign Terrorist Organizations," http://www.state.gov/j/ct/rls/other/des/123085.htm.

248 Larry Niksch and Raphael Perl, "North Korea: Terrorism List Removal?," *CRS Report for Congress RL30613* (11 December 2007), 18. A 2008 Congressional Research Service report provides additional information on North Korea's alleged arms sales to the Tamil Tigers. *See* Larry Niksch, "North Korea: Terrorism List Removal?," *CRS Report for Congress RL30613* (06 November 2008), 23-24.

The reports of North Korea's pre-2008 support for Hezbollah were not mentioned in any of the U.S. State Department's annual terrorism reports, but they have been tested in federal court. In 2010, thirty plaintiffs sued North Korea in the U.S. District Court for the District of Columbia, for personal injury arising from Hezbollah's 2006 rocket attacks against civilian targets in northern Israel.[249] The plaintiffs named North Korea as a defendant, alleging that it had provided training and technical assistance to Hezbollah. They also alleged that North Korea had "provided rocket and missile components" to Iran, "where, pursuant to a prior agreement between Iran, North Korea and Hezbollah, they were assembled and shipped to Hezbollah in Lebanon."[250]

One of the plaintiffs described the injuries he suffered as a consequence of the rocket attacks that followed:

> 34. On July 13, 2006, at approximately 14:30, plaintiff Michael Fuchs was driving his car in Safed when a rocket fired by Hezbollah at Safed struck nearby. Massive amounts of shrapnel penetrated Fuchs' car and caused him severe injuries. Fuchs lost large quantities of blood, lost consciousness and was rushed to the intensive care unit of Rebecca Ziv Hospital. Fuchs' throat was slashed as a result of the explosion and his right hand remains completely paralyzed. Fuchs has been permanently disabled. He is unable to work and relies on intensive and expensive medical treatments on an on-going basis.[251]

On July 23, 2014, U.S. District Judge Royce Lamberth of the U.S. District Court for the District of Columbia ruled in favor of the plaintiffs, finding "clear and convincing evidence" of North Korea's support for Hezbollah.

> The Court finds by clear and convincing evidence that Hezbollah carried out the rocket attacks that caused plaintiffs' injuries and that North Korea provided material support. Prior to July 12, 2006, North Korea provided Hezbollah with a wide variety of material support and resources, within the meaning of 28 U.S.C. § 1605A. This material support included professional military and intelligence training and assistance in building a massive network

---

249   First Amended Complaint, *Kaplan v. Hezbollah*, Civil Action No. 09-646 (RWR) (D.D.C. Dec. 15, 2009).

250   *Id.* at 10-11.

251   *Id.* at 12.

of underground military installations, tunnels, bunkers, depots and storage facilities in southern Lebanon. Moreover, North Korea worked in concert with Iran and the Syria [*sic*] to provide rocket and missile components to Hezbollah. North Korea sent these rocket and missile components to Iran where they were assembled and shipped to Hezbollah in Lebanon via Syria. These rocket and missile components were intended by North Korea and Hezbollah to be used and were in fact used by Hezbollah to carry out rocket and missile attacks against Israeli civilian targets. Between July 12, 2006 and August 14, 2006, Hezbollah fired thousands of rockets and missiles at civilians in northern Israel. As a result of North Korea's provision of material support and resources, Hezbollah was able to implement and further goals shared by Hezbollah and North Korea.[252]

The court has since appointed a special master to apportion damages among the plaintiffs.

K. 2003–2008: SHIFT AWAY FROM JUSTIFICATIONS FOR LISTING

Despite the revelations about North Korea's abductions and proliferation, the U.S. State Department's 2003 annual report language softened so perceptibly as to suggest a disharmony between the U.S. State Department and other senior Bush Administration officials, whose public statements did not suggest that de-listing was imminent.

The 2003 report again asserted that "[t]he Democratic People's Republic of Korea (DPRK) is not known to have sponsored any terrorist acts since the bombing of a Korean Airlines flight in 1987." It praised North Korea for "laying the groundwork for a new position on terrorism by framing the issue as one of 'protecting the people,'" for meeting with the Prime Minister of Japan on the abduction issue, and for "trying to resolve" its harboring of the Japanese Red Army hijackers. Ultimately, however, the report faulted Pyongyang for its failure to take "substantial steps to cooperate in efforts to combat international terrorism."[253]

---

252   *Kaplan v. Cent. Bank of the Islamic Republic of Iran*, Civil Action No. 10-483 (RCL), 4-5 (D.D.C. July 23, 2014).

253   U.S. Department of State, *Patterns of Global Terrorism: 2003*, 91-92.

By 2004, the U.S. State Department's annual report had pupated to something resembling its present form. It noted the return of five surviving Japanese abductees, but acknowledged that many other cases remained unresolved, and that DNA tests had proven that remains returned to Japan by North Korea were not, in fact, the remains of the abductees, as represented by Pyongyang.[254]

L. 2007: Construction of a Nuclear Reactor at Al-Kibar, Syria

In September 2007, multiple news sources reported that the Israeli Air Force had bombed a remote site in the Syrian desert, near the city of Deir-az-Zour.[255] Syria has been listed as a state sponsor of terrorism since 1979.[256] It soon emerged that the site was a nuclear reactor, that North Korea had provided substantial assistance in the design and construction of the plant, and that the plant's design closely resembled that of the North Korean reactor at Yongbyon.

According to some reports, the reactor was destroyed shortly before it was to be loaded with fuel rods and brought online. After the Israeli air strike, the Syrian government quickly buried the reactor's remains.

The Israeli attack came at a sensitive moment, just five months after North Korea signed an agreement with the Bush Administration, agreeing to dismantle its nuclear programs. Rep. Jane Harman, the Chairwoman of the House Homeland Security Subcommittee on Intelligence, and Rep. Peter Hoekstra, the Ranking Member of the House Intelligence Committee, both initially accused the Bush Administration of withholding intelligence from them about Al-Kibar.[257]

In 2008, the Central Intelligence Agency released a video, describing the evidence of North Korea's involvement in the Al-Kibar reactor project. The video made the following assertions:

254   U.S. Department of State, Office of the Coordinator for Counterterrorism, *Country Reports on Terrorism 2004* (April 2005), http://www.state.gov/documents/organization/45313.pdf, 90.

255   *See* Allen Thomson, "A Sourcebook on the Israeli Strike in Syria, 6 September 2007," *Federation of American Scientists*, last modified 09 January 2015, http://fas.org/man/eprint/syria.pdf.

256   Holly Fletcher, "State Sponsor: Syria," *Council on Foreign Relations*, last modified 01 February 2008, http://www.cfr.org/syria/state-sponsor-syria/p9368.

257   "Transcripts: CNN Late Edition with Wolf Blitzer," *CNN*, 21 October 2007, http://transcripts.cnn.com/TRANSCRIPTS/0710/21/le.01.html.

Syria was building a gas-cooled, graphite-moderated reactor that was nearing operational capability in August 2007. The reactor would have been capable of producing plutonium for nuclear weapons, was not configured to produce electricity and was ill-suited for research. The reactor was destroyed in early September 2007 before it was loaded with nuclear fuel or operated. We are convinced based on a variety of information that North Korea assisted Syria's covert nuclear activities both before and after the reactor was destroyed. Only North Korea has built this type of reactor in the past 35 years.[258]

According to the Congressional Research Service, U.S. intelligence agencies concluded that "the reactor's purpose was to produce plutonium for nuclear weapons." The report also cited a 2013 U.S. State Department report, noting that Al-Kibar was isolated from any civilian population, was not configured for power production, and was not well suited for research. The report concluded that Syria had built Al-Kibar to produce plutonium with "North Korean assistance."[259]

The International Atomic Energy Agency (IAEA) was denied access to the Al-Kibar site until June 2008. In 2011, the IAEA concluded that the site was "very likely a nuclear reactor," an assertion the Syrian government denies.[260]

M. 2006-2008: NORTH KOREA'S REMOVAL FROM THE SSOT LIST

On February 13, 2007, Assistant Secretary of State Christopher Hill and his North Korean counterpart, Kim Kye-gwan, signed an agreement for the phased denuclearization of North Korea. As a term of the agreement, the United States agreed to "begin the process" of removing North Korea from the list of state sponsors of terrorism:

> 3. The DPRK and the U.S. will start bilateral talks aimed at resolving bilateral issues and moving toward full diplomatic relations. The U.S. will begin the process of removing the designation of the DPRK as a state sponsor of terrorism, and advance the process of

---

258   Mario Profaca, "CIA video showing suspected Syrian nuclear reactor," *YouTube* video, 6:03, 25 April 2008, https://www.youtube.com/watch?v=yj62GRd0Te8.

259   Paul K. Kerr, Mary Beth D. Nikitin and Steven A. Hildreth, "Iran-North Korea-Syria Ballistic Missile and Nuclear Cooperation," *CRS Report for Congress R43480* (16 April 2014), 6-7.

260   *Id.* at 6.

terminating the application of the Trading with the Enemy Act with respect to the DPRK.[261]

The U.S. State Department published its 2006 country reports on terrorism shortly thereafter, on April 30, 2007. The discussion of North Korea's sponsorship of terrorism consisted of four terse sentences:

> The Democratic People's Republic of Korea (DPRK) was not known to have sponsored any terrorist acts since the bombing of a Korean Airlines flight in 1987. The DPRK continued to harbor four Japanese Red Army members who participated in a jet hijacking in 1970. The Japanese government continued to seek a full accounting of the fate of the 12 Japanese nationals believed to have been abducted by DPRK state entities; five such abductees have been repatriated to Japan since 2002. In the February 13, 2007 Initial Actions Agreement, the United States agreed to "begin the process of removing the designation of the DPRK as a state-sponsor of terrorism."[262]

Although the Japanese government objected to North Korea's removal from the SSOT list without a resolution of the abduction issue, by 2007, "[t]he Bush Administration increasingly took the position that the issue of North Korea's kidnapping of Japanese citizens was not linked to removing North Korea from the terrorism list, from the standpoint of U.S. law or policy."[263]

Despite delays in implementing the agreement, questions about the veracity of North Korea's nuclear program declarations, and the revelation of the Al-Kibar reactor in Syria, President Bush signed a notice of his intention to remove North Korea from the SSOT list on June 26, 2008. The half-page notice certified, as required by section 6(j)(4)(B) of the Export Administration Act, that North Korea had not "provided any support for international terrorism during the preceding 6-month period," and had "provided assurances that it will not support acts of international terrorism in the future."[264] Because of the congressional notice and 45-day waiting period

---

261   "Text of the agreement on North Korea's nuclear disarmament," *Associated Press*, 13 February 2007.

262   U.S. Department of State, Office of the Coordinator for Counterterrorism, *Country Reports on Terrorism 2006* (April 2007), http://www.state.gov/documents/organization/83383.pdf, 147.

263   Larry Niksch, "Summary" in "North Korea: Terrorism List Removal?," *CRS Report for Congress RL30613* (06 November 2008).

264   "Certification of Rescission of North Korea's Designation as a State Sponsor of Terrorism: Memorandum for the Secretary of State," 73 Fed. Reg. 37351 (July 1, 2008).

mandated by Section 6(j)(4)(B),[265] the removal of North Korea did not become effective until October 11, 2008.[266]

The decision was controversial. It drew strong opposition from Congress, particularly from its Republican members,[267] and also strained U.S. relations with Japan.[268] Presidential candidates John McCain and Barack Obama both gave qualified support for the de-listing, but conditioned their support on verification of North Korea's continued disarmament. Then-Senator Obama issued the following statement on June 26, 2008, after President Bush announced his decision to remove North Korea from the list:

> The declaration has not yet been made available, so Congress has not had a chance to review it. Before weighing in on North Korea's removal from the list of state sponsors of terrorism, Congress must take the next 45 days to examine the adequacy of the North Korean declaration and verification procedures. Sanctions are a critical part of our leverage to pressure North Korea to act. They should only be lifted based on North Korean performance. If the North Koreans do not meet their obligations, we should move quickly to re-impose sanctions that have been waived, and consider new restrictions going forward.[269]

Separately, Senator Obama called the decision "an appropriate response, as long as there is a clear understanding that if North Korea fails to follow through there will be immediate consequences." He continued, "If North Korea refuses to permit robust verification, we should lead all members of the Six-Party Talks in suspending energy assistance, re-imposing sanctions that have recently been waived, and considering new restrictions."[270]

---

265   Larry Niksch and Raphael Perl, "North Korea: Terrorism List Removal?," *CRS Report for Congress RL30613* (06 April 2007), 11.

266   U.S. Department of State, *Country Reports on Terrorism 2008*, 181.

267   Daniel W. Reilly, "House Republicans blast Bush for North Korea decision," *Politico*, 26 June 2008.

268   Blaine Harden and Robin Wright, "U.S. to Delist North Korea As Sponsor of Terrorism," *The Washington Post*, 27 June 2008.

269   "Statement of Senator Barack Obama on the North Korean declaration," *The New York Times*, 26 June 2008.

270   "U.S. takes North Korea off terror list," *CNN*, 11 October 2008.

IV. Post-2008 Support for Acts of Terrorism

When President Bush removed North Korea from the SSOT list in October 11, 2008, he made two certifications under Section 6(j)(4)(B) of the Export Administration Act[271]—that North Korea had not provided any support for international terrorism during the preceding 6-month period, and that it had provided assurances that it would not support acts of international terrorism in the future. At the time, North Korea continued to harbor four Japanese Red Army hijackers, had not accounted for eight of the Japanese citizens it previously admitted to abducting, but committed itself to begin bilateral talks with Japan to settle the "unfortunate past and the outstanding issues of concern."[272] Arguably, these actions are continuing offenses until North Korea resolves them. Both issues remain unresolved, and subsequent events have cast doubt on the sincerity of North Korea's 2007 commitments.

The most significant change in the U.S. State Department's reporting on North Korea since 2008 is not to its content, but to its placement. Starting in 2009, the country-specific reporting about North Korea was moved from the section on state sponsors of terrorism to the regional section on East Asia and the Pacific. There have been some year-to-year variations in the language in the U.S. State Department's annual terrorism reports. The U.S. State Department's 2012 report, for example, noted North Korea's failure to cooperate with counterterrorism efforts, and its deficient regimes to combat money laundering and terrorist financing.

The U.S. State Department's reports, however, have frequently failed to mention conduct that meets the definitions of international terrorism, or which is similar to conduct cited in other U.S. State Department reports on the state sponsorship of terrorism. The evidence suggests that North Korea began to expand its sponsorship of terrorism significantly shortly before its removal from the SSOT list in 2008. Section IV of this report describes North Korea's post-2008 conduct that, if confirmed, would fit the legal definitions of "international terrorism" or "terrorist activity." These include material support for Foreign Terrorist Organizations, international assassinations (both attempted and executed), and international abductions.

Section V describes North Korea's post-2008 conduct that is similar to conduct supporting the SSOT listing of North Korea and other governments. For organizational reasons, the 2014 threat

---

271   Export Administration Act of 1979, Pub. L. No. 96-72, § 6(j)(4)(B) added by Pub. L. No. 101-222, § 4, 103 Stat. 1897.

272   Paul Kerr, "Initial Pact Reached to End North Korean Nuclear Weapons Program," *Arms Control Today*, 01 March 2007.

by North Korean hackers against American moviegoers, which also fits the legal definition of international terrorism, is discussed in Section V.

Despite this increase in North Korea's sponsorship of terrorism, the U.S. State Department's discussion of North Korea in its annual *Country Reports on Terrorism* has remained largely unchanged. A comparison of the U.S. State Department's 2005 report, when North Korea was still designated as an SSOT,[273] reveals it to be nearly identical to the U.S. State Department's 2013 report,[274] except that the 2005 report mentions South Korean and third-country nationals held by North Korea.

A. 2009–2014: Suspected Arms Transfers to Terrorists

In 2009, multiple interceptions of North Korean shipments to Iran and its terrorist clients evidenced the importance of North Korea's role as a supplier of arms to terrorists backed by Iran. News reports have alleged that these arms were destined for Iran's terrorist clients, including Hezbollah and Hamas. A 2010 Congressional Research Service report cites Israeli and Lebanese news reports, which in turn quote "Western intelligence sources," concluding that "most of" the North Korean weapons seized in 2009 "likely were bound for Hezbollah."[275]

In November 2009, *Bloomberg News* quoted a 2009 UN POE report alleging that North Korea operated a "highly sophisticated international network for the acquisition, marketing and sale of arms and military equipment" that had become "one of the country's principal sources for obtaining foreign exchange," and a source of funding for its nuclear weapons programs.[276] In 2011, Larry Niksch, formerly with the Congressional Research Service, estimated that Pyongyang earned "between $1.5 billion and $2 billion annually" from its dealings with Iran, including arms sales to Iranian-backed terrorists.[277]

These conclusions are consistent with the findings of the District Court in the *Kaplan v. Hezbollah* litigation, that Iran had arranged for North Korea to supply weapons to Hezbollah though Syria (*supra* Section III.J).

---

273   U.S. Department of State, *Country Reports on Terrorism 2005*, 175.

274   U.S. Department of State, *Country Reports on Terrorism 2013*, 62.

275   Larry A. Niksch, "North Korea: Terrorism List Removal," *CRS Report for Congress RL30613* (06 January 2010), http://fpc.state.gov/documents/organization/137273.pdf, 18.

276   Bill Varner, "North Korea Arms Trade Funds Nuclear-Bomb Work, UN Panel Says," *Bloomberg*, 18 November 2009.

277   Larry A. Niksch, "When North Korea Mounts Nuclear Warheads on Its Missiles," *The Journal of East Asian Affairs* 25.2 (Fall/Winter 2011), 7.

Joshua Stanton

1. 2009: M/V *ANL AUSTRALIA* ARMS SEIZURE

In July of 2009, the United Arab Emirates seized a cargo of North Korean weapons bound for Iran aboard the M/V *ANL Australia*. By this time, UN Security Council resolutions prohibited North Korea from selling any arms and related materiel.[278] Initially, the UAE authorities found "rocket launchers, detonators, munitions and ammunition for rocket-propelled grenades" inside a container.[279] According to *The Washington Post*, however, the "real find" was concealed deeper inside the ship's hold: "hundreds of crates containing military hardware and a grayish, foul-smelling powder, explosive components for thousands of short-range rockets." The discovery "raised fears that Iran is ramping up efforts to arm itself and anti-Israel militias in the Middle East."

> Among the weapons components discovered aboard the ANL Australia were 2,030 detonators for 122mm rockets, as well as electric circuitry and a large quantity of solid-fuel propellant, according to an account given by UAE and UN Security Council officials. The materials were bought from North Korea and shipped halfway around the globe in sealed containers, labeled as oil-drilling supplies, that passed through a succession of freighters and ports.[280]

The weapons were loaded onto the *ANL Australia* in Shanghai[281] and "arranged by the Shanghai office of an Italian [shipping] company."[282]

The *Post*'s report also claimed that "[s]imilar caches were discovered this year at a port in Cyprus and aboard Russian and German cargo ships searched by U.S. Navy teams." It reported that the *ANL Australia* was just one of "five vessels caught this year carrying large, secret caches of weapons apparently intended for the Lebanese group Hezbollah, the Palestinian organization Hamas or

---

278   "Security Council, Acting Unanimously, Condemns in Strongest Terms Democratic People's Republic of Korea Nuclear Test, Toughens Sanctions," U.N. Press Release SC/9679 (12 June 2009) at http://www.un.org/press/en/2009/sc9679.doc.htm.

279   Louis Charbonneau, "UAE seized N.Korea arms shipment bound for Iran," *Reuters*, 28 August 2009.

280   Joby Warrick, "Arms smuggling heightens Iran fears," *The Washington Post*, 03 December 2009.

281   *Id.*

282   Louis Charbonneau, "UAE seized N.Korea arms shipment bound for Iran," *Reuters*, 28 August 2009.

the Quds Force, a wing of the Iranian Revolutionary Guard Corps that supports insurgents in Iraq." According to the *Washington Post*, not all of these shipments contained North Korean weapons.[283]

A separate report by *The Guardian* quotes U.S. officials as alleging that the *ANL Australia* "was one of five vessels caught this year carrying large consignments of weapons apparently intended for Iran's militia clients such as Hezbollah and Hamas, or for the al-Quds brigade of Iran's Revolutionary Guard."[284]

2. 2009: M/V *Francop* Arms Seizure

In March 2014, a UN POE monitoring the enforcement of sanctions against North Korea reported that in November 2009, the Israeli Navy intercepted a 500-ton shipment of 122-millimeter artillery rockets aboard the M/V *Francop*, which was bound for Latakia, Syria.[285]

The UN report found that the rockets and their markings bore strong similarities to the weapons seized at Bangkok and Abu Dhabi, leading it to conclude that it was "highly likely" that the weapons found aboard the *Francop* were produced in North Korea, too.[286]

According to the UN report, the weapons were being "shipped by the Islamic Republic of Iran to the Syrian Arab Republic" and "may have originated in the Democratic People's Republic of Korea."[287] The Israeli government alleged that the weapons were being shipped to Hezbollah.[288] Hezbollah denied any link to the shipment.[289]

---

283   Joby Warrick, "Arms smuggling heightens Iran fears," *The Washington Post*, 03 December 2009.

284   Simon Tisdall, "North Korean plane carrying smuggled arms seized in Thailand," *The Guardian*, 13 December 2009.

285   Report of the UN POE established pursuant to resolution 1874 (2009), para. 108, U.N. Doc. S/2014/147 (2014) at http://www.un.org/ga/search/view_doc.asp?symbol=S/2014/147.

286   *Id.* at para. 110.

287   *Id.* at para. 108.

288   Richard Boudreaux, "Israel says its navy intercepted 300 tons of weapons headed for Hezbollah," *Los Angeles Times*, 05 November 2009.

289   Amy Teibel, "Hezbollah denies link to arms ship," *Associated Press*, 05 November 2009.

As noted in Section II.E.1, the U.S. State Department cited the seizure of the M/V *Francop* in support of Syria's SSOT listing. It did not cite the seizure in any of its annual "Country Reports" about North Korea, however.

3. 2009: Seizure of Weapons Shipment at Bangkok

In December 2009, a chartered Il-76 transport aircraft was intercepted at Bangkok while en route from Pyongyang to Iran.[290] A 2013 UN POE report found that although the aircraft's declared cargo was "mechanical parts," its hold was loaded with "35 tons of conventional arms and munitions, including 240-mm rockets, rocket-propelled grenades and man-portable air defence systems, valued at over US$ 16 million."[291]

[Man-portable surface-to-air missiles, intercepted at Bangkok. Image Credit: UN POE[292]]

The UN POE called the shipment "a clear violation" of the UN's North Korea sanctions resolutions.[293] The flight crossed through Chinese airspace.[294] The UN POE reported the existence

---

290   "Thailand seizes 'arms plane flying from North Korea," *BBC News*, 12 December 2009.

291   Report of the UN POE established pursuant to resolution 1874 (2009), para. 75, U.N. Doc. S/2013/337 (2013) at http://www.un.org/ga/search/view_doc.asp?symbol=S/2013/337.

292   *Id.* at 33, Figure XVIII.

293   *Id.* at para. 75.

294   Nicholas Kralev, "China fails to stop illegal North Korean arms shipments," *The Washington Times*, 17 December 2009.

of "numerous flight plans filed for the outbound and projected return route of the aircraft," suggesting that additional shipments may have been planned.[295] In May of 2010, Israeli Foreign Minister Avigdor Lieberman alleged that North Korea and Iran had the "intention to smuggling [*sic*] these weapons to Hamas and to Hezbollah."[296]

Congress is sufficiently concerned about the proliferation of man-portable surface-to-air missiles (MANPADS) to terrorists that it has declared that "it should be the policy of the United States to hold foreign governments accountable for knowingly transferring MANPADS to state-sponsors of terrorism or terrorist organizations."[297] This provision requires the President to impose sanctions on the transferring government. The sanctions imposed, however, are a subset of the sanctions consequential to a SSOT listing—including bans on most foreign assistance and military-related exports—that would be unlikely to have a material impact on North Korea.

4. 2011: Production of Ballistic Missiles in Syria; Alleged Delivery to Hezbollah

In July 2011, *The Times* (UK) reported that Syria had constructed a factory to produce SCUD-D ballistic missiles, which are "assembled with the help of North Korean experts" at a factory near Hama.[298] According to the report, ten of the missiles, which have a range of 430 miles, were delivered to Hezbollah.[299]

5. 2014: Reported Agreement to Sell Rockets to Hamas

In July 2014, shortly after the end of sustained fighting between Israel and Hamas, *The Telegraph*, citing "Western security sources," reported that Hamas had agreed to purchase communications equipment and artillery rockets from North Korea. The sources reported that the deal, worth hundreds of thousands of dollars, would be handled through intermediaries in Lebanon. The report alleged that Hamas had already made an initial payment to Pyongyang,

---

295   Report of the UN POE established pursuant to resolution 1874 (2009), para. 64, U.N. Doc. S/2010/571 (2010) at http://www.un.org/ga/search/view_doc.asp?symbol=S/2010/571.

296   "Israel says seized North Korean arms were for Hamas, Hezbollah," *Reuters*, 12 May 2010.

297   Department of State Authorities Act of 2006, Pub. L. No. 109–472, § 12, 120 Stat. 3558.

298   Nicholas Blanford, Sheera Frenkel and Richard Beeston, "Embattled Syrian regime still sending missiles to Lebanese militants," *The Times*, last modified 15 July 2011.

299   "Syria Arming Hizbollah In Lebanon," *Fox9.com*, 14 July 2011.

and hoped that weapons would soon begin to arrive in Gaza to replenish stocks that had been fired into Israel.

The Telegraph report also cited Israeli military commanders, who alleged that North Korea has provided Hamas with technical assistance on the construction of its tunnel system.[300]

In March 2014, the UN POE stated that the fuse of a 333-millimeter rocket found in Israel bore "some similarities with fuses produced in the Democratic People's Republic of Korea previously seized."[301, 302]

6. Analysis

If these reports are accurate, these arms transfers would meet the historical and legal standards for support for acts of international terrorism.

The U.S. State Department has designated Hamas and Hezbollah as Foreign Terrorist Organizations.[303] The U.S. State Department has not designated the Quds Force as a Foreign Terrorist Organization, but the Treasury Department designated the Quds Force under Executive Order 13,224[304] in 2007 for "providing material support to the Taliban and other terrorist organizations."[305] Iran has been designated as a state sponsor of terrorism since 1984, and Syria has been designated since 1979.[306]

---

300   Con Coughlin, "Hamas and North Korea in secret arms deal," *The Telegraph*, 26 July 2014.

301   Report of the UN POE established pursuant to resolution 1874 (2009), para. 111, U.N. Doc. S/2014/147 (2014).

302   A January 2015 report by the Congressional Research Service cites a post on the Arms Control Wonk blog showing Hamas fighters in possession of North Korean-made anti-tank guided missiles. *See* Mark E. Manyin et al., "North Korea: Back on the State Sponsors of Terrorism Lists?," *CRS Report for Congress R43865* (21 January 2015), http://www.fas.org/sgp/crs/row/R43865.pdf, 14.

303   U.S. Department of State, "Foreign Terrorist Organizations," http://www.state.gov/j/ct/rls/other/des/123085.htm.

304   U.S. Department of State, Office of the Coordinator for Counterterrorism, "Executive Order 13224," 23 September 2001, http://www.state.gov/j/ct/rls/other/des/122570.htm.

305   U.S. Department of the Treasury, "Fact Sheet: Designation of Iranian Entities and Individuals for Proliferation Activities and Support for Terrorism," 25 October 2007, http://www.treasury.gov/press-center/press-releases/Pages/hp644.aspx.

306   U.S. Department of State, "State Sponsors of Terrorism," http://www.state.gov/j/ct/list/c14151.htm.

The provision of weapons to Hamas or Hezbollah would fit within the categories of conduct described in Section II.D and also fits the plain meaning of "support for acts of international terrorism." The U.S. State Department has repeatedly cited arms transfers to Foreign Terrorist Organizations in its annual reporting on the state sponsorship of terrorism (*supra* Section II.E.1). The statutory provision that establishes the annual terrorism reporting requirement also requires the U.S. State Department to report on "significant military or paramilitary training or transfer of weapons by foreign governments to" Foreign Terrorist Organizations,[307] strongly suggesting that "support" includes the provision of arms to Foreign Terrorist Organizations.

Although a recent Congressional Research Service report questioned[308] whether North Korea knew that terrorists were the end users of the arms,[309] a previous Congressional Research Service report cited "a large body of reports describe a long-standing, collaborative relationship between North Korea and the Iranian Revolutionary Guard Corps."[310] The *Kaplan* decision (*supra* Section III.J) also establishes that before the 2009 seizures, North Korea had a long-standing pattern and practice of supporting Hezbollah with training, technical support, and arms sales.

The statutes do not require evidence that the supplier state knew or intended that the arms be delivered to a terrorist organization to merit SSOT listing; however, the preponderance of the evidence suggests that North Korea knew that it was providing weapons to terrorist organizations.

B. 2008–2014: ASSASSINATIONS, KIDNAPPING, ATTEMPTS, AND PLOTS

By the time a UN Commission of Inquiry convened to investigate human rights in North Korea, the North Korean government had demonstrated its ability to intimidate North Korean refugees, and that it was willing to assassinate both refugees and the South Korean activists who assisted them. Some of this intimidation used threats of harm to refugees' family members. In 2012, for example, *The Washington Post* reported that a North Korean refugee was forced to

---

307 Foreign Relations Authorization Act for Fiscal Years 1988 and 1989, Pub. L. No. 100-204, § 140(b)(2)(B), 101 Stat. 1348 (as amended).

308 Mark E. Manyin et al., "North Korea: Back on the State Sponsors of Terrorism Lists?," *CRS Report for Congress R43865* (21 January 2015), 14.

309 FRAA Section 140(b)(3)(B) requires reporting of a state's "transfer of weapons by foreign governments to" terrorist groups, notwithstanding the government's knowledge that terrorists would be the end users of the weapons.

310 Larry Niksch, "Summary" in "North Korea: Terrorism List Removal?," *CRS Report for Congress RL30613* (06 November 2008).

return to North Korea because of threats to her son and his family.[311] The refugee later delivered a confession at a government-staged news conference in Pyongyang. North Korean agents seek information about the identities of North Korean refugees living in South Korea.[312] North Korean clandestine agents have a long history of abducting refugees and dissidents abroad.[313] According to recent reports,[314] North Korean agents operate on Chinese soil,[315] where they kidnap North Korean refugees.[316]

As a consequence, many North Korean refugees continue to fear for their safety, or for the safety of their families, even after finding refuge in South Korea and other countries. When the UN Commission of Inquiry took evidence of human rights violations in North Korea, "[m]ore than 80 witnesses and experts testified publicly."[317] Most of these witnesses were North Korean. The Commission also took "240 confidential interviews with victims and other witnesses"[318] because of "the fear of reprisals by witnesses."[319] The Commission's report stated, "Most of the potential witnesses residing outside the State were afraid to testify, even on a confidential basis, because they feared for the safety of family members and assumed that their conduct was still being clandestinely monitored by the authorities."[320]

311   Chico Harlan, "Behind North Korea's propaganda star, a darker story," *The Washington Post*, 22 September 2012.

312   Joseph Fitsanakis, "Korea spy gave North data on 10,000 defectors living in South," *IntelNews*, 22 January 2013.

313   Andrei Lankov, "Body snatching, North Korean style," *Asia Times Online*, 26 February 2005.

314   Hyung-jin Kim, "Prosecutors arrest SKorean for spying for NKorea," *Associated Press*, 11 April 2010.

315   Lee Jong-heon, "Deep-cover North Korean spies in Seoul," *UPI*, 29 August 2008.

316   "Seoul detains 'North Korean refugee hunter'," *BBC News*, 12 April 2010.

317   UN Human Rights Council report of the commission of inquiry on human rights in the Democratic People's Republic of Korea, para. 12, U.N. Doc. A/HRC/25/63 (2014) at http://www.ohchr.org/Documents/HRBodies/HRCouncil/CoIDPRK/Report/A.HRC.25.63.doc.

318   *Id.* at para. 14.

319   *Id.* at para. 19.

320   *Id.*

1. 2008: Assassination Plot Against South Korean Military Officer

In October 2008, Won Jeong-hwa, a female North Korean spy who had previously worked in China targeting and abducting refugees,[321] was convicted and sentenced to a five-year prison term by a South Korean court for her attempt to assassinate "a South Korean military officer in Hong Kong using an aphrodisiac laced with poison."[322] Won was also carrying poisoned needles, which she was ready to jab into "South Korean intelligence agents" when ordered to do so.[323]

Because the targets of this plot were military personnel, it could be argued that Won's plans were not classifiable as terrorism, but Won's plans appear to have involved the assassination of unarmed, off-duty military personnel (*supra* Section II.E.5). Won's possession of poison needles is also consistent with other North Korean attempts to assassinate civilians over the next three years.

Won was also reported to have attempted to arrange a meeting with Hwang Jang-yop, the highest-ranking official to have defected from North Korea, and the target of a subsequent North Korean assassination attempt.[324]

2. 2010: Attempts To Assassinate Hwang Jang-yop

In April 2010, South Korean authorities announced that they had arrested two North Korean agents who posed as defectors while plotting to assassinate Hwang Jang-yop. Following his 1997 defection, Hwang had become a fierce critic of the North Korean regime, and received multiple death threats.[325]

---

321   John M. Glionna and Youkyung Lee, "A seductress who had an ear for secrets," *Los Angeles Times*, 07 October 2008.

322   "North Korean spy jailed in sex-for-secrets case," *NBC News*, 15 October 2008.

323   "North Korea's 'Sex for Secrets' Poison Needle Plotter Sentenced to 5 Years," *Associated Press*, 15 October 2008.

324   "North Korean spy jailed in sex-for-secrets case," *NBC News, op. cit.*

325   Choe Sang-hun, "South Korea Arrests 2 From North in Alleged Assassination Plot," *The New York Times*, 21 April 2010.

In June of 2010, Major Kim Myong-ho and Major Dong Myong-gwan[326] of the RGB pled guilty to the assassination plot in a South Korean court.[327] The court sentenced each of the defendants to ten years in prison. The defendants told prosecutors that Lt. Gen. Kim Yong-chol, the head of the RGB, personally assigned them to the assassination mission in November of 2009.

[Lt. Gen. Kim Yong-Chol. Image Credit: *KCNA*, via *North Korea Leadership Watch*[328]]

On October 10, 2010, just six months after the failure of the assassination plot, Hwang Jang-yop died, apparently of natural causes, at the age of 87. Ten days later, South Korea announced that it had arrested another North Korean agent, Ri Dong-sam, who was also plotting to murder Hwang. Police denied the existence of any connection between that arrest and Hwang's death.[329]

3. 2011: Assassination of Kim Chang-hwan in Dandong, China

Kim Chang-hwan, also known as Patrick Kim, was "a human rights activist who secretly helped people slip out of North Korea into China."[330] In August 2011, Kim was waiting for a taxi in the

---

326   Sometimes rendered as Tong Myung-gwan and Kim Myung-ho, or Dong Con-gwan and Kim Yong-ho.

327   Park Si-soo, "A peek into North Korean spies in courtroom," *The Korea Times*, 16 June 2010.

328   "Biographies: Gen. Kim Yong Chol," North Korea Leadership Watch, https://nkleadershipwatch.wordpress.com/leadership-biographies/lt-gen-kim-yong-chol/.

329   "S Korea arrests 'N Korean agent'," *Al Jazeera*, 20 October 2010.

330   Barbara Demick, "North Korea suspected in poison-needle attacks," *Los Angeles Times*, 09 October 2011.

Chinese city of Dandong,[331] when he suddenly fell to the ground while foaming at the mouth. He was found with "a discolored complexion, spots on his fingers and limbs, flecks of foam on his mouth,"[332] and died before arriving at the hospital.[333]

Kim's family suspected North Korean agents of his murder, but the South Korean Foreign Ministry did not initially confirm whether it believed that North Korea was involved in the attacks.[334] It said that the Chinese government had conducted an autopsy and had found no traces of poison. The Seoul Central District Court ordered prosecutors to investigate the attacks. In December 2012, the *Korea Times* reported that the prosecutors had concluded that North Korean agents were behind Kim's murder.

> According to the court ruling, in March 2010 the North Korean agent was ordered to keep an eye on Kim who was helping North Koreans defect to the South. The agent in question contacted Kim by pretending to be a defector, and reported Kim's activities to the North's intelligence agency.[335]

According to the report, the agents murdered Kim with neostigmine bromide,[336] a powerful toxin loaded into syringes disguised as pens.

4. 2011: ATTEMPTED ASSASSINATION OF ACTIVIST IN YANJI, CHINA

The *L.A. Times* also reported that a North Korean agent was suspected in an attack against another South Korean activist, in the city of Yanji, China, a day after the murder of Patrick Kim. The unidentified activist reported that while he was standing at an intersection, "he felt a pinprick in his lower back." "As he collapsed, he heard a man muttering behind him in Chinese, 'Sorry, sorry.'" This time, the victim survived.[337]

---

331   "North Korean Agents Suspected In 'Poison Needle' Attacks In China," *AFP*, 09 September 2011.

332   "S. Korean missionary dies near Chinese border with N. Korea," *Yonhap News*, 09 September 2011.

333   Barbara Demick, "North Korea suspected in poison-needle attacks," *op. cit.*

334   "North Korean Agents Suspected In 'Poison Needle' Attacks In China," *AFP*, *op. cit.*

335   Kim Rahn, "Missionary poisoned by NK agent," *The Korea Times*, 07 December 2012.

336   "Material Safety Data Sheet: Neostigmine Bromide," *TCI America*, 26 February 2005, https://www.spectrumchemical.com/MSDS/TCI-N0358.pdf.

337   Barbara Demick, "North Korea suspected in poison-needle attacks," *op. cit.*

5. 2011: ATTEMPTED ASSASSINATION OF PARK SANG-HAK

Park Sang-hak may be the most controversial North Korean refugee and activist in South Korea. Park, a former North Korean ruling party official, leads a group known as the Fighters for a Free North Korea, which launches helium balloons filled with anti-regime leaflets from South Korea into North Korea.[338] In September 2011, South Korea's National Intelligence Service announced that it had foiled a plot by a North Korean agent, later identified as An Hak-young, to assassinate Park, using a poisoned needle.[339] The National Intelligence service released a photograph of the needle.[340] A South Korean press report claims that this needle also contained neostigmine bromide.[341]

[Poison needle exhibited by South Korean authorities, allegedly seized from North Korean assassin. Image Credit: *CNN*[342]]

338   David Feith, "Park Sang Hak: North Korea's 'Enemy Zero'," *The Wall Street Journal*, 05 July 2013.

339   Ashley Rowland and Yoo Kyong Chang, "South Korea court upholds prison term for would-be assassin," *Stars and Stripes*, 29 November 2012.

340   Andy Campbell, "Poison Pen, Flashlight Gun Among North Korean Assassin's Toolkit," *The Huffington Post*, 26 November 2012.

341   Kim Rahn, "Missionary poisoned by NK agent," *op. cit.*

342   Paula Hancocks and K.J. Kwon, "'Poison' pen mightier than sword for would-be North Korean assassin," *CNN*, 26 November 2012.

In November 2012, An was sentenced to a four-year prison term for the attempt. An, who defected in 1995, claimed that the North Korean government recruited him by offering him "money and a better life for his family members who still lived in the North."[343]

6. 2014: ATTEMPTED KIDNAPPING OF A NORTH KOREAN STUDENT IN FRANCE

In November 2014, according to multiple published reports, North Korean government agents attempted to kidnap a North Korean student in Paris.[344] One account alleged that the attempted kidnapping was motivated by the student's family relationship with an official linked to Jang Song-taek, who was purged in December 2013.[345] The attempt failed when the student escaped from his captors at Charles De Gaulle Airport. The captors intended to put him aboard a flight to Pyongyang.[346] "A French source with knowledge of the case" confirmed an attempt to kidnap a North Korean student, but did not confirm the North Korean government's involvement.[347]

7. ANALYSIS

Section 140 of the Foreign Relations Authorization Act for Fiscal Years 1988 and 1989 defines "international terrorism" as "premeditated, politically motivated violence perpetrated against noncombatant targets by subnational groups or clandestine agents … involving the citizens or the territory of more than 1 country."[348] The attacks and plots described above all appear to have been politically motivated, premeditated acts by North Korean clandestine agents against noncombatant targets. They would therefore fit this definition.

Under INA § 212(a)(3)(B)(iii), attacks and plots by North Korean clandestine agents against noncombatant targets would be "unlawful under the laws of the place where it is committed" and would involve the use of an "explosive, firearm, or other weapon or dangerous device …

---

343   Ashley Rowland and Yoo Kyong Chang, "South Korea court upholds prison term for would-be assassin," *op. cit.*

344   "Son of Jang Song-thaek's aide disappears in Paris," *Yonhap News*, 19 November 2014.

345   Koo Jun Hoe, "Son of Purged Aide Escapes Forced Repatriation to NK," *Daily NK*, 20 November 2014.

346   John Lichfield, "Audacious North Korean kidnap plot foiled at Paris airport as 'Asian men' attempted to bundle student onto plane," *The Independent*, 23 November 2014.

347   Elaine Ganley, "North Korean Student Escapes Kidnap Attempt In Paris," *Associated Press*, 22 November 2014.

348   Foreign Relations Authorization Act, Fiscal Years 1988 and 1989, Pub. L. No. 100-204, § 140(d), 101 Stat. 1349 (as amended).

with intent to endanger, directly or indirectly, the safety of one or more individuals or to cause substantial damage to property."[349] None of the targets would likely be viewed as legitimate military targets, including the South Korean military officers targeted by Won Jeong-hwa,[350] who presumably would have been unarmed and off-duty when attacked. As such, the attacks and plots would also fit the definition of "terrorist activity."

The U.S. State Department's annual reports on terrorism also provide substantial precedent for classifying an attack by North Korean clandestine agents against dissidents and refugees abroad as acts of terrorism (*supra* Section II.E.4).

V. Other Conduct That Could Justify SSOT Re-Listing

The U.S. State Department's annual reports on terrorism have cited several categories of conduct that do not fit within the legal definitions of "international terrorism" or "terrorist activity" to support or justify SSOT listings (*supra* Section II.E.7). North Korea has also engaged in several of these categories of conduct.

In other cases, North Korean conduct that has been cited as a possible basis for SSOT listing does not clearly fit within either of the legal definitions or the U.S. State Department precedent for conduct justifying a SSOT listing. In such cases, it is for Congress to decide whether to clarify, narrow, or expand the legal standards for SSOT listing, or to decide that the conduct should be sanctioned under some other basis (*infra* Section VI).

A. 2009: Nuclear and Missile Tests

Although WMD development does not fit any of the legal definitions of "international terrorism," the U.S. State Department has repeatedly cited it as a basis for the SSOT listings of Iran, Syria, Libya (*supra* Section II.E.7), and North Korea (*supra* Section III.G). North Korea's agreement to dismantle its nuclear programs was the justification for North Korea's removal from the SSOT list (*supra* Sections III.K & III.M). Thus, notwithstanding the strict legal definitions, a state's possession and development of WMD technology has historically been, and continues to be, a significant factor in the U.S. State Department's SSOT reporting.

---

349   Immigration and Nationality Act, Pub. L. No. 82-414, § 212(a)(3)(B)(ii) added by Pub. L. No. 101-649, § 601(a), 104 Stat. 5067 (as amended by Pub. L. No. 107-56, § 411(a)(1), 115 Stat. 345).

350   John M. Glionna and Youkyung Lee, "A seductress who had an ear for secrets," *op. cit.*

By the time President Obama was inaugurated on January 21, 2009, President Bush's nuclear disarmament agreement with North Korea had broken down over verification protocols. On February 24, 2009, North Korea announced that it would test a long-range Taepodong-2 ballistic missile. It conducted that test on April 5, 2009. On May 25, 2009, North Korea conducted its second underground nuclear test. Since 2009, North Korea has carried out numerous rocket and missile tests, and at least one additional nuclear test, in February 2013.[351]

The tests caused some senators to demand North Korea's re-listing as an SSOT. In 2009, Republicans John McCain and Sam Brownback joined with Democrat Evan Bayh to add a "sense of the Senate" amendment to the Defense Authorization Bill recounting North Korea's recent missile tests, its expulsion of nuclear inspectors, its support for Hezbollah, and its nuclear proliferation to Syria.[352] The amendment called on President Obama to re-list North Korea as a state sponsor of terrorism, but was defeated after Senator John Kerry, then the Chairman of the Foreign Relations Committee, offered a competing amendment requiring the U.S. State Department to study the question of North Korea's re-listing.[353]

Since 2008, the U.S. State Department has not cited North Korea's nuclear weapons, or its ballistic missile development or testing, in its annual "Country Reports," although it has repeatedly and recently cited the WMD development and proliferation of Iran and Syria, which have longstanding military ties to North Korea (*supra* Sections II.E.7, III.G, and IV.A).

B. 2009-2014: PROLIFERATION OF NUCLEAR AND CHEMICAL WEAPONS TECHNOLOGY

Following North Korea's February 2013 nuclear test, *The New York Times* quoted a "senior American official" who said, in reference to Iran, "[I]t's very possible that the North Koreans are

---

351   In May 2010, North Korea claimed to have produced nuclear fusion. At least two scientific studies have noted surges in radioisotopes and radionuclides in the atmosphere following this claim, and a Chinese scientist recently claimed to have found seismic evidence of a small test. *See* "Global Security Newswire: Isotope Analysis Points to Two North Korean Nuclear Test Detonations in 2010," *Nuclear Threat Initiative*, 07 February 2012; Michael Schoeppner and Ulrich Kühn, "Improve the nuclear test monitoring system," *Bulletin of the Atomic Scientists*, 09 February 2015; and "N. Korea 'conducted small-yield nuclear explosion' in 2010: China professor," *Yonhap News*, 04 December 2014.

352   Amendment 1597 to S. 1390, 111th Cong. (2009).

353   Brian Faler, "Senate Asks Obama to Consider Adding North Korea to Terror List," *Bloomberg*, 22 July 2009.

testing for two countries."[354] No compelling evidence of this relationship has been published in open sources, however.

On June 12, 2009, the UN Security Council approved Resolution 1874,[355] which prohibited North Korea from exporting "all arms and related materiel, as well as … financial transactions, technical training, advice, services or assistance related to the provision, manufacture, mainte-nance or use of such arms or materiel."[356] Following the passage of this resolution, a UN POE established by the Security Council began to issue reports on North Korea's violations of the Security Council resolutions.

Reports by the UN POE from 2010,[357] 2012,[358] 2013,[359] and 2014[360] document numerous examples of North Korea's efforts to procure or sell equipment and materials for ballistic missiles, chemical weapons, or nuclear weapons programs. Many of the weapons seized were destined for listed state sponsors of terrorism, including Iran and Syria, or for the terrorist groups themselves. Often, the POE's reports included photographs of the items seized while on their way to or from North Korea. This paper will not repeat the details of those exhaustive reports, but will high-light or supplement a few of their relevant findings.

Since 2012, the UN POE has published evidence that North Korea has provided assistance to Syria's chemical weapons program. On September 12, 2011, a member state informed the UN

354   David E. Sanger and Choe Sang-hun, "North Korea Confirms It Conducted 3rd Nuclear Test," *The New York Times*, 11 February 2013.

355   The Security Council would later approve Resolutions 2087 and 2094 in 2013, following a ballistic missile test and a third underground nuclear test. *See* Security Council resolution 2087, U.N. Doc. S/RES/2087 (22 January 2013) at http://www.un.org/ga/search/view_doc.asp?symbol=S/RES/2087(2013); and "Security Council Strengthens Sanctions on Democratic People's Republic of Korea, in Response to 12 February Nuclear Test," U.N. Press Release SC/10934 (07 March 2013) at http://www.un.org/press/en/2013/sc10934.doc.htm.

356   "Security Council, Acting Unanimously, Condemns in Strongest Terms Democratic People's Republic of Korea Nuclear Test, Toughens Sanctions," U.N. Press Release SC/9679 (12 June 2009).

357   Report of the UN POE established pursuant to resolution 1874 (2009), U.N. Doc. S/2010/571 (2010).

358   Report of the UN POE established pursuant to resolution 1874 (2009), U.N. Doc. S/2012/422 (2012) at http://www.un.org/ga/search/view_doc.asp?symbol=S/2012/422.

359   Report of the UN POE established pursuant to resolution 1874 (2009), U.N. Doc. S/2013/337 (2013).

360   Report of the UN POE established pursuant to resolution 1874 (2009), U.N. Doc. S/2014/147 (2014).

that in November 2009, it intercepted four containers aboard a merchant vessel filled with 13,000 chemical protective coats, and 23,600 gas indicator ampules to detect the presence of chemical weapons.[361] A consistent press report suggests that the member state was Greece.[362] The POE inspected the items and found them to be similar to other, previously seized items of known North Korean origin. For example, the POE found (paragraph 62) that the protective coats were "identical to those seized in October 2009 on board the MSC *Rachele*."[363] The *Rachele* was intercepted by the South Korean Coast Guard,[364] brought to Busan, inspected, and found to be carrying chemical protective clothing.[365]

 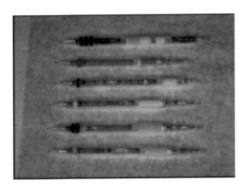

[Gas mask and gas indicator ampules seized by Greek authorities in November 2009. Image Credit: 2012 UN POE report (S/2012/422), Figure XI, page 29.]

Because neither shipment contained protective boots, the POE inferred that "one or several other shipments may have escaped seizure." Both shipments originated in the North Korean port of Nampo, were trans-shipped through China, and were on their way to Latakia, Syria. In April 2013, Turkish authorities found a third shipment,[366] containing North Korean-made gas masks, aboard the M/V *El Entisar*.[367]

---

361   Report of the UN POE established pursuant to resolution 1874 (2009), para. 65, U.N. Doc. S/2012/422 (2012).

362   Paul Eckert, "Specter of North Korea lurks in U.S. debate on Syria's chemical weapons," *Reuters*, 05 September 2013.

363   Report of the UNN POE established pursuant to resolution 1874 (2009), para. 65, U.N. Doc. S/2012/422 (2012).

364   Joseph S. Bermudez Jr., "North Korea's Chemical Warfare Capabilities," *38 North*, 10 October 2013.

365   "Seized North Korean Containers Held Nuclear or Chemical Suits," *Handy Shipping Guide*, 07 October 2009.

366   Joseph S. Bermudez Jr., "North Korea's Chemical Warfare Capabilities," *op. cit.*

367   "North Korea 'tried to export gas masks to Syria'," *AFP*, 27 August 2013.

Joshua Stanton

In February 2013, Israeli aircraft struck a North Korea-linked research center near Damascus. Although the target was a shipment of anti-aircraft missiles, *The New York Times* described the center as Syria's "main research center for work on biological and chemical weapons."[368]

In June 2013, the conservative South Korean daily, *The Chosun Ilbo*, reported that North Korea was playing "a decisive role in arming the Syrian regime with chemical weapons," by providing it with vacuum dryers "used to dry liquid chemical materials to make them into fine powder" and "after-sales services."[369]

President Obama has accused the Syrian government of using chemical weapons in the civil war that broke out in 2011. A Pentagon spokesman has credited the possibility of North Korean assistance to Syria's chemical weapons program.[370]

[Syrian children, allegedly killed by a regime chemical weapons attack. Image credit: *AP*/Local Committee of Arbeen[371]]

---

368   David E. Sanger, Erich Schmitt, and Jodi Rudoren, "Israeli Strike Into Syria Said to Damage Research Site," *The New York Times*, 03 February 2013.

369   "N.Korea 'Exporting Chemical Weapons Parts to Syria'," *The Chosun Ilbo*, 17 June 2013.

370   Lee Chi-dong, "Pentagon suspects NK-Syria ties on chemical weapons," *Yonhap News*, 06 September 2013.

371   Erika Solomon and Stephen Kalin, "Syrians retrieve 'sleeping' dead after alleged chemical attack kills more than 500 people, including scores of children," *National Post*, 21 August 2013.

Despite strong evidence of North Korea's support for Syria's chemical weapons program, no open-source evidence links this proliferation directly or indirectly to any Foreign Terrorist Organization. As noted in Section III.G above, FRAA Section 140 requires the U.S. State Department to report annually on states that harbor terrorists and that fail "to prevent the proliferation of and trafficking in weapons of mass destruction in and through the territory of the country." Arguably, the U.S. State Department should be reporting on North Korea's WMD proliferation because, by the U.S. State Department's own admission, Pyongyang is harboring four Japanese Red Army hijackers. The U.S. State Department has historically reported on states' proliferation-related activities, even without direct evidence that the governments in question were proliferating that technology to terrorists (*supra* Section II.E.7).

Although the proliferation of weapons of mass destruction among state sponsors of terrorism does not fit the legal definitions of "international terrorism" or "terrorist activity," the U.S. State Department has repeatedly cited military assistance to state sponsors of terrorism in its annual "Country Reports." The U.S. State Department's 2012 and 2013 reports also cite Iran's provision of weapons, funds, and training to Syrian military forces since the beginning of the Syrian Civil War in 2011. As noted in Section II.E.7, the U.S. State Department has also cited defense and diplomatic cooperation with state sponsors of terrorism, including both Iran and Syria, to support its SSOT designations.

Consequently, a recent Congressional Research Service report concludes that North Korea's transfer of chemical weapons-related materials to Syria "conceivably could have met the criteria for re-listing as a state sponsor of terrorism."[372] Although this is a more difficult conclusion to reach than it is for the conduct described in Section IV, there is sufficient precedent in U.S. State Department reports to support it.

Section VI of this report addresses the question of whether WMD proliferation should be sanctionable under some other, more logically appropriate, authority.

---

372   Mark E. Manyin et al., "North Korea: Back on the State Sponsors of Terrorism Lists?," *CRS Report for Congress R43865* (21 January 2015), 14.

C. 2010, 2014: Direct Attacks Against South Korea

1. 2010: Sinking of the ROKS *Cheonan*

On March 26, 2010, the South Korean naval corvette *Cheonan* exploded and sank, killing 46 sailors. On May 20, 2009, an international investigation group determined that a torpedo fired by a North Korean submarine sank the *Cheonan*.[373]

Following the release of the report, members of Congress again began to call for North Korea to be re-listed as a SSOT; however, *The Washington Post* blog, The Cable, reported that the administration viewed the SSOT list as "overly politicized" and "more trouble than it's worth."[374]

[Image Credit: Agencies, via *China Daily*[375]]

North Korea denied responsibility for the attack, accusing South Korea of orchestrating it to escalate tension.[376]

---

373   The Joint Civilian-Military Investigation Group, "Investigation Result on the Sinking of ROKS 'Cheonan'," 20 May 2010 at http://news.bbc.co.uk/nol/shared/bsp/hi/pdfs/20_05_10jigreport.pdf.

374   Josh Rogin, "The Cable: Zimbabwe ambassador heckles U.S. official; N. Korea on terror list?," *The Washington Post*, 27 May 2010.

375   "South Korea mourns victims of sunken warship," *China Daily*, 28 April 2010, http://www.chinadaily.com.cn/photo/2010-04-28/content_9782137.htm.

376   "'Cheonan' Case Is Product of US-S. Korea Conspiracy—Rodong Sinmun," *KCNA* 28 March 2011.

2. 2014: SHELLING OF YEONPYEONG ISLAND

On November 24, 2010, North Korea shelled the island of Yeonpyeong, including the civilian village located on the island. The attack killed two South Korean civilians, and two Republic of Korea Marines.[377] Yeonpyeong Island is one of several South Korean islands in the Yellow Sea that lie within waters claimed by both North and South Korea. North Korea said that the attack was in response to South Korean live-fire exercises in waters it claimed.[378]

[Destroyed civilian homes on Yeonpyeong Island. Image Credit: *Kyodo/Reuters*[379]]

On December 6, 2010, Luis Moreno Ocampo, the former Prosecutor of the International Criminal Court, announced that his office has begun a "preliminary examination" of whether the attack

---

377   Mark McDonald, "'Crisis Status' in South Korea After North Shells Island," *The New York Times*, 23 November 2010.

378   "S. Korean Authorities' Talk about 'Sincerity' Nonsensical," *KCNA*, 17 March 2011.

379   "South Korea orders more troops to front line," *NBC News*, 25 November 2010.

was a war crime.[380] In June 2012, Fatou Bensouda of the Gambia, a nation that enjoys close relations with North Korea, succeeded Ocampo.[381] On June 23, 2014, Bensouda announced that her office had determined that the North Korean shelling of Yeonpyeong Island "was directed at a lawful military target" and did not meet the definition of a war crime.[382]

3. 2014: Cross-Border Attack Against Leaflet Launches

On October 10, 2014, North Korean defector and activist Park Sang-hak, a previous target of an assassination attempt by North Korean agents in South Korea (*supra* Section IV.B.5), launched 33 balloons carrying 1.5 million anti-Kim Jong-un leaflets near the Demilitarized Zone between North and South Korea. Although Park and other defector-led organizations had conducted numerous, similar launches in the past, and despite the fact that the balloons carried no dangerous cargo, North Korea fired on the balloons with 14.5-millimeter anti-aircraft guns.[383]

It was the first time since the shelling of Yeonpyeong Island in 2010 that North Korea had fired into South Korean territory using weapons other than small arms (as previously used in minor skirmishes). The incident did not cause any injuries or damage.[384] The Republic of Korea Army responded by firing .50 caliber (12.7-millimeter) machine guns toward the North Korean gun positions. North Korea demanded that South Korea block future leaflet launches.

4. Analysis

The attacks of 2010 caused some members of Congress to call for North Korea to be re-listed as an SSOT. On June 28, 2010, a reporter asked Philip J. Crowley, the Assistant Secretary of the Bureau of Public Affairs, whether North Korea would be re-designated as a state sponsor of terrorism as a consequence of its sinking of the *Cheonan*. Crowley responded that "[a]s a

---

380   International Criminal Court, Office of the Prosecutor, "ICC Prosecutor: alleged war crimes in the territory of the Republic of Korea under preliminary examination," 06 December 2010.

381   Bensouda announced her determination two weeks after a meeting between the Gambian and North Korean Foreign Ministers in Banjul. *See* "Talks between FMs of DPRK and Gambia Held," *KCNA*, 08 June 2014.

382   "Statement of the Prosecutor of the International Criminal Court, Fatou Bensouda, on the conclusion of the preliminary examination of the situation in the Republic of Korea," ICC Press Release 1019, 23 June 2014.

383   Oh Seok-min, "Two Koreas exchange gun fire after S. Korea's anti-Pyongyang campaigns," *Yonhap News*, 10 October 2014.

384   Kang Jin-kyu, "North shoots at balloon launches along the DMZ," *Korea JoongAng Daily,* 10 October 2014.

general matter, a state military attack on a military target would not be considered an act of international terrorism."[385]

FRAA Section 140 defines "international terrorism" as "premeditated, politically motivated violence perpetrated against noncombatant targets by *subnational groups or clandestine agents* ... involving the citizens or the territory of more than 1 country."[386] Under this definition, the bombardment of Yeonpyeong Island by the North Korean armed forces would not be considered "international terrorism," despite its indiscriminate targeting and killing of civilians. The attack on the ROKS *Cheonan* is a slightly less clear case, because it was allegedly the work of clandestine agents of the RGB (*supra* Section II.E.6); however, the attackers were operating from a naval vessel, using conventional military arms.

There is more room for argument under the definition of "terrorist activity." To qualify as "terrorist activity" under INA § 212(a)(3)(B)(iii), an attack must be "unlawful under the laws of the place where it is committed" and must involve the use of an "explosive, firearm, or other weapon or dangerous device ... with intent to endanger, directly or indirectly, the safety of one or more individuals or to cause substantial damage to property."[387] Although North and South Korea are two states in a technical state of war, there were no ongoing hostilities at the time of either attack.

Precedent from prior U.S. State Department reports would not support a classification of the *Cheonan* attack as terrorism, because it was directed against on-duty military personnel. As such, it would not meet the standard that the U.S. State Department has applied to attacks against military personnel (*supra* Section II.E.5). With respect to the 2010 Yeonpyeong attack and the 2014 cross-border firing on the leaflet balloons, there is no precedent for the U.S. State Department classifying a conventional military attack as terrorism.

All three of the attacks described in Section V.C are more plausibly described as acts of war than as acts of terrorism. All three attacks were unprovoked and unjustified, threatened international peace, and drew only a limited response from the United States, South Korea, or the United Nations. This report's Conclusions and Recommendations address the issue of

---

385   U.S. Department of State, "North Korea: State Sponsor of Terrorism? (Taken Question)," last modified 28 June 2010, http://www.state.gov/r/pa/prs/ps/2010/06/143720.htm.

386   Foreign Relations Authorization Act, Fiscal Years 1988 and 1989, § 140(d), 101 Stat. 1349 (as amended). [Emphasis added].

387   Immigration and Nationality Act, Pub. L. No. 82-414, § 212(a)(3)(B)(ii) added by Pub. L. No. 101-649, § 601(a), 104 Stat. 5067 (as amended by Pub. L. No. 107-56, § 411(a)(1), 115 Stat. 345).

whether these attacks, which do not clearly fit within the various definitions of "terrorism," should instead be sanctionable under some other, more appropriate authority (*infra* Section VI).

D. 2009-2014: Threats Against Civilian Targets in South Korea

North Korea's threats of violence against the South Korean government and civilian targets are so frequent that they seldom attract widespread media interest in the United States today. North Korea's official *Korean Central News Agency*, or *KCNA*, publishes most of these threats. The threats were often conditioned on some potential alleged "provocation" by the United States or South Korea, but were frequently phrased vaguely enough that the precise nature of the "provocation" was not clear. In other cases, the threats were conditioned on lawful acts, such as the enforcement of UN Security Council sanctions, or defensive military exercises. What follows is a partial list of those threats.

Many of the threats implied the use of direct, conventional military force, which would put them outside the legal and precedential definitions of "international terrorism," despite their apparent intent to "intimidate or coerce a civilian population" or a government.[388]

On March 5, 2009, in response to annual U.S.-South Korean military exercises, *KCNA* announced that the North Korean military was "compelled to declare that security cannot be guaranteed for south Korean civil airplanes flying through the territorial air of our side and its vicinity, its territorial air and its vicinity above the East Sea of Korea, in particular, while the military exercises are under way."[389] The South Korean Ministry of Unification denounced the threat: "To militarily threaten the normal operations of civil airplanes not only violates international rules but is also an inhumane act that can never be justified."[390] The threat caused civil air traffic to be rerouted away from North Korean airspace.

In April 2012, a *KCNA* article stated that a "special operation action group" would "reduce all the ratlike groups and the bases for provocations to ashes in three or four minutes, in much shorter time, by unprecedented peculiar means and methods of our own style." It also threatened South Korean broadcasters and newspapers and television stations, which it accused of "destroying the mainstay of the fair public opinion." It concluded, "The special actions of our revolutionary armed forces will start soon to meet the reckless challenge of the group of traitors."[391]

---

388   18 U.S.C. § 2331(1).

389   "U.S. and S. Korean Puppets Warned Not to Act Rashly," *KCNA*, 05 March 2009.

390   Kim Hyun, "S. Korea says N. Korea's warning on flights against int'l law inhumane," *Yonhap News*, 06 March 2009.

391   Choe Sang-hun, "North Korea Threatens South With Military Action," *The New York Times,* 23 April 2012.

In May 2012, *KCNA* published the following banner images:

[Images from *KCNA*, collected by the author.]

In June 2012, in response to press reports critical of the North Korean government, *KCNA* published a lengthy "ultimatum" against three South Korean newspapers (*The Chosun Ilbo, The Joongang Ilbo,* and The *Dong-A Ilbo*) and four broadcasting networks (*KBS, CBS, MBC,* and *SBS*). The threat included the (mostly incorrect[392]) coordinates of the newspapers' offices in Seoul:

> Officers and men of the army corps, divisions and regiments on the front and strategic rocket forces in the depth of the country are loudly calling for the issue of order to mete out punishment, declaring that they have already targeted Chosun Ilbo at coordinates of 37 degrees 56 minutes 83 seconds North Latitude and 126 degrees 97 minutes 65 seconds East Longitude in the Central District, Seoul, Choongang Ilbo at coordinates of 37 degrees 33 minutes 45 seconds North Latitude and 126 degrees 58 minutes 14 seconds East Longitude in the Central District, Seoul, the Dong-A Ilbo at coordinates of

---

392   Evan Ramstad, "North Korea's Threat Gets Coordinates Wrong," *The Wall Street Journal*, 05 June 2012.

37 degrees 57 minutes 10 seconds North Latitude and 126 degrees 97 minutes 81 seconds East Longitude in Jongro District, Seoul, KBS, CBS, MBC and SBS, the strongholds of the Lee group orchestrating the new vicious smear campaign.

In view of this grave situation the KPA General Staff sends the following ultimatum to the Lee group of traitors:

The revolutionary armed forces of the DPRK are the army of the supreme commander and the people's army which is devotedly defending the supreme commander and protecting his idea and the people and children whom he values and loves so much.

It is the iron will of the army of the DPRK that the dens of heinous provocateurs hurting the dignity of the supreme leadership of the DPRK and desecrating its idea, system and people should not be allowed to exist as they are.

We would like ask the Lee group if it wants leave all this to be struck by the DPRK or opt for apologizing and putting the situation under control, though belatedly.

It should take a final choice by itself.

Now it is impossible for the officers and men of the KPA three services to keep back their towering resentment any longer. In case dens of monstrous crimes are blown up one after another, the Lee group will be entirely held responsible for this.

If the Lee group recklessly challenges our army's eruption of resent-ment, it will retaliate against it with a merciless sacred war of its own style as it has already declared.

We are fully ready for everything.

Time is running out.[393]

---

393   "General Staff of KPA Sends Open Ultimatum to S. Korean Group of Traitors," *KCNA*, 04 June 2012.

In March 2013, North Korea's quasi-official news service *Uriminzokkiri*, which is reportedly based in China, warned the civilian populations of Baekryeong Island, Yeonpyeong Islands, and other islands in the Yellow Sea to evacuate their homes.[394] It threatened to "wipe out" the largest of them, Baekryeong Island, which has a population of 5,000.[395] That same month, North Korea threatened to launch a "pre-emptive nuclear strike" against the United States.[396]

On November 23, 2014, *KCNA*, referring to South Korea's vote for a resolution of the Third Committee of the UN General Assembly,[397] criticizing North Korea's human rights record, published an article containing the following language:

> We would like to question the Park Geun Hye group busy billing the adoption of the above-said "resolution" as a sort of a significant event. Does she think Chongwadae will be safe if guns roar for aggression and a nuclear war breaks out on the Korean Peninsula? Can she prolong her remaining days in America after leaving south Korea? ...
>
> Japan, political pigmy, would be well advised to behave itself properly, cogitating about what miserable end it will meet.
>
> Once a sacred war is launched to protect the sovereignty of the DPRK, not only the U.S. but the Park Geun Hye group and Japan will have to be hit hard and sent to the bottom of the sea ...
>
> The UN also can never evade the responsibility for the catastrophic consequences entailed by what happened there. All this is the DPRK's response to the "human rights" racket of the U.S.-led hostile forces.[398]

---

394   "North Korea tells South to leave islands," *BBC News*, 16 March 2013.

395   "NKorea threatens to 'wipe out' SKorean island," *The Sydney Morning Herald*, 13 March 2013.

396   Paul Eckert, "Analysis: Behind North Korea bluster, a record of troubling actions," *Reuters*, 07 March 2013.

397   Situation of human rights in the Democratic People's Republic of Korea, U.N. doc. A/C.3/69/L.28/Rev.1 (2014) at http://www.un.org/Docs/journal/asp/ws.asp?m=A/C.3/69/L.28/Rev.1.

398   "KPA and People Will Not to Tolerate 'Human Rights' Racket of U.S. and Its Allies: NDC of DPRK," *KCNA*, 23 November 2014.

Although the U.S. State Department has previously cited states' threats of violence by their *clandestine* forces against non-combatants in support of SSOT listings (*supra* Section II.E.3), it has not previously described threats to use conventional military force against noncombatants as "international terrorism." These threats, therefore, would not fit the FRAA Section 140 definition of "international terrorism," which applies only to the acts of "subnational groups" and "clandestine agents."[399]

These threats do, nonetheless, reach both the plain meaning of "terrorize," and the concerns at the heart of the SSOT authorities. Military threats of unprovoked attacks against civilian airliners, newspapers, and governments are a serious threat to international peace, to freedom of expression, and to the human rights of South Koreans. Section VI of this report addresses the question of whether these threats should be sanctionable under some other, more logically appropriate, authority.

E. 2010–2014: MONEY LAUNDERING AND TERRORIST FINANCING

As noted in Section II.E.7, the U.S. State Department has repeatedly cited countries' deficient anti-money laundering (AML) and combating-the-financing-of-terrorism (CFT) regimes in its annual reporting on governments listed as state sponsors of terrorism.

The principal international body charged with evaluating and enforcing AML and CFT standards is the Financial Action Task Force, or FATF, "an inter-governmental body established in 1989" by the finance ministers of its member states "to set standards and promote effective implementation of legal, regulatory and operational measures for combating money laundering, terrorist financing and other related threats to the integrity of the international financial system."[400]

Although the FATF's recommendations do not bind member states,[401] they are influential enough to help "generate the necessary political will to bring about national legislative and

---

399   Foreign Relations Authorization Act, Fiscal Years 1988 and 1989, § 140(d), 101 Stat. 1349 (as amended).

400   Financial Action Task Force, "About us: Who we are," http://www.fatf-gafi.org/pages/aboutus/.

401   Financial Action Task Force, "The FATF Recommendations,"
http://www.fatf-gafi.org/topics/fatfrecommendations/documents/fatf-recommendations.html.

regulatory reforms in these areas."[402] These recommendations have also been recognized in UN Security Council resolutions, including at least one Chapter VII resolution specific to North Korea.[403]

Beginning in February 2010, the FATF began to issue warnings about North Korea's AML and CFT deficiencies, and called on its members to "consider the risks" to "the international financial system" arising from these deficiencies before doing business with North Korea. It also called on North Korea to "work with the FATF to develop a viable AML/CFT regime in line with international standards."[404] The FATF re-issued this warning in June[405] and October of 2010.[406]

On February 25, 2011, the FATF first called on members to put in place "countermeasures" against North Korea's abuse of the financial system. This warning imposed the strictest category of advisory applicable to any jurisdiction, placing North Korea in the same category as Iran. The FATF called on member governments "to advise their financial institutions to give special attention to business relationships and transactions with the DPRK, including DPRK companies and financial institutions," "to apply effective counter-measures to protect their financial sectors from money laundering and financing of terrorism … risks emanating from the DPRK," and to "protect against correspondent relationships being used to bypass or evade counter-measures and risk mitigation practices." Finally, the FATF called on member states to consider money laundering and terrorist-financing risks "when considering requests by DPRK financial institutions to open branches and subsidiaries" in their jurisdictions.[407]

---

402   Financial Action Task Force, "About us: Who we are," http://www.fatf-gafi.org/pages/aboutus/.

403   "Security Council Strengthens Sanctions on Democratic People's Republic of Korea, in Response to 12 February Nuclear Test," U.N. Press Release SC/10934 (07 March 2013).

404   Financial Action Task Force, "Public Statement," 18 February 2010, http://www.fatf-gafi.org/documents/documents/fatfpublicstatement-february2010.html.

405   Financial Action Task Force, "Public Statement," 25 June 2010, http://www.fatf-gafi.org/documents/documents/fatfpublicstatement-25june2010.html.

406   Financial Action Task Force, "Public Statement," 22 October 2010, http://www.fatf-gafi.org/documents/documents/fatfpublicstatement-22october2010.html.

407   Financial Action Task Force, "Public Statement," 25 February 2011, http://www.fatf-gafi.org/documents/documents/fatfpublicstatement-25february2011.html.

Since February 2011, the FATF has re-issued its call for "countermeasures" against North Korea on multiple occasions, most recently on October 24, 2014.[408]

On March 7, 2013, following North Korea's third nuclear test, the UN Security Council recognized the FATF's advisories in the preamble to Resolution 2094. The resolution's key financial provisions mirrored FATF advisories, directing member states to take actions consistent with those advisories; requiring "enhanced monitoring" of North Korean transactions; and restricting bulk cash transfers, correspondent accounts, and new branches and subsidiaries of North Korean financial institutions.[409]

Recently, North Korea has made overtures to the FATF indicating a willingness to adopt improved AML and CFT regimes. In July 2014, the Asia/Pacific Group on Money Laundering, a regional coalition with an associate membership in the FATF, granted North Korea "observer" status.[410] In January 2015, *KCNA* announced that North Korea's Central Bank had "committed itself to implementing the action plan of 'international standard' for anti-money laundering and combating the financing of terrorism."[411]

As of February 2015, however, North Korea's overtures had not resulted in greater financial transparency, materially significant cooperation with FATF, or the amendment of its laws and regulations relevant to AML and CFT. On February 27, 2015, the FATF renewed its call for countermeasures against North Korean money laundering, and stated that despite the North Korean government's outreach, "the FATF remains concerned by [North Korea's] failure to address the significant deficiencies in its anti-money laundering and combating the financing of terrorism (AML/CFT) regime and the serious threat this poses to the integrity of the international financial system."[412]

---

408   Financial Action Task Force, "Public Statement," 24 October 2014, http://www.fatf-gafi.org/documents/documents/public-statement-oct2014.html.

409   "Security Council Strengthens Sanctions on Democratic People's Republic of Korea, in Response to 12 February Nuclear Test," U.N. Press Release SC/10934 (07 March 2013).

410   "N. Korea to discuss anti-money laundering efforts with int'l body," *Yonhap News*, 23 July 2014.

411   "DPRK Will Honor Its Commitments to Anti-Money Laundering," *KCNA*, 16 January 2015.

412   Financial Action Task Force, "Public Statement," 27 February 2015, http://www.fatf-gafi.org/documents/news/public-statement-february-2015.html.

Although a state's failure to enact sufficient AML and CFT measures may be an appropriate matter for discussion in annual U.S. State Department reporting, it is a passive omission rather than an affirmative act of support for international terrorism. Without evidence that a government willfully facilitates or tolerates terrorist financing, it should not be a basis to find that a state has "repeatedly provided support for acts of international terrorism."

Furthermore, the law already provides an effective legal deterrent for insufficient AML and CFT safeguards under Section 311 of the USA PATRIOT Act.[413] The Treasury Department has previously designated Iran as a Primary Money Laundering Concern (PMLC) under this authority, for its deceptive financial practices in support of terrorism and proliferation.[414] A PMLC designation triggers enhanced due diligence and reporting requirements for a designated bank or jurisdiction, and can completely sever a PMLC's access to the global financial system. Sufficient evidence exists[415] to justify a PMLC designation of North Korea.[416]

F. 2009–2014: Cyberattacks

The cyberattacks and threats against Sony Pictures Entertainment Inc. have again revived the debate over North Korea's SSOT listing. Following President Obama's attribution of the attack and threat to North Korea, some influential members of Congress have expressed support for re-listing North Korea as a SSOT. In January 2015, Democratic Senator Bob Menendez, the outgoing Chairman of the Senate Foreign Relations Committee, called on the Secretary of State to re-list North Korea.[417] Rep. Ileana Ros-Lehtinen of Florida also announced that she would introduce legislation calling for North Korea's restoration to the list.[418] Rep. Ed Royce (R, Cal.), Chairman of the House Foreign Affairs Committee, has also supported North Korea's re-listing.[419]

---

413   31 U.S.C. § 5318A.

414   Department of the Treasury: Notice of Finding, 76 Fed. Reg. 72756 (Nov. 25, 2011).

415   Department of the Treasury: Final Rule, 72 Fed. Reg. 12730 (Mar. 19, 2007).

416   "US Targeting Secret Funds of North Korea's Kim," *Voice of America*, 15 April 2013.

417   "Transcripts: State of the Union with Candy Crowley," *CNN*, 04 January 2015, http://transcripts.cnn.com/TRANSCRIPTS/1501/04/sotu.01.html.

418   "U.S. congresswoman vows bill listing N.K. as terror sponsor," *Yonhap News*, 06 January 2015.

419   Matthew Pennington and Eric Tucker, "Are tougher U.S. sanctions against North Korea the right call after Sony hack?," *PBS Newshour*, 19 December 2014.

In a briefing before that Committee on January 13, 2015, several other members of both parties called for or suggested that North Korea should be re-designated as an SSOT.[420]

1. 2009–2013: Suspected Cyberattacks Against Banks, Websites, Newspapers, Broadcasters

In 2009, at least 35 U.S. and South Korean government and commercial websites were hit by cyberattacks. The targets of the attacks included the websites of "the departments of Homeland Security and Defense, the Federal Aviation Administration and the Federal Trade Commission," and *The Washington Post*.[421] South Korean intelligence officials told South Korean newspapers that they suspected North Korea of being behind the attacks; however, *The New York Times* later reported that although "many suspected North Korea, a clear link to the country was never established."[422]

In May 2011, South Korea accused North Korea of being behind a cyberattack against Nonghyup Bank. South Korea called the attack "cyber-terror" and a "provocation upon our society."[423] North Korea denied responsibility for the attack.[424] In June 2012, South Korea's *The Joongang Ilbo* reported that it was the victim of a cyberattack.[425] Once again, North Korea was suspected, but no clear link to North Korea was ever established. The cyberattack coincided closely in time with the North Korean threat against South Korean newspapers, including *The Joongang Ilbo*, described in section V.D.

---

420   "North Korea Threat Assessment," *C-SPAN*, 13 January 2015, http://www.c-span.org/video/?323725-1/ hearing-north-korean-cyber-nuclear-threats.

421   Ellen Nakashima, Brian Krebs and Blaine Harden, "U.S., South Korea Targeted in Swarm of Internet Attacks," *The Washington Post*, 09 July 2009.

422   Choe Sang-hun, "Computer Networks in South Korea Are Paralyzed in Cyberattacks," *The New York Times*, 20 March 2013.

423   "North Korea hackers blamed for bank crash in South," *Global Post,* 04 May 2011.

424   "DPRK denies cyber attack on Nonghyup Bank," *North Korea Tech*, 11 May 2011, http://www.northkoreatech. org/2011/05/11/dprk-denies-cyber-attack-on-nonghyup-bank/.

425   "South Korean paper hit by major cyber attack," *AFP*, 11 June 2012.

In March 2013, *The New York Times* reported that cyberattacks "paralyzed" three South Korean banks and two television broadcasters.[426] *The Wall Street Journal* reported that the networks' broadcasts continued despite the attacks.[427] Although South Korea did not attribute the attack to North Korea at the time, the *Times* quoted unnamed experts who blamed North Korean hackers based in China. The attack featured malware known as "Dark Seoul,"[428] which was first identified in 2012, and which the FBI would later cite as a comparator to the malware used to attack Sony Pictures Entertainment Inc. in 2014. On January 13, 2015, Ambassador Sung Kim, Special Representative for North Korea Policy and Deputy Assistant Secretary for Korea and Japan, stated in a briefing before the House Foreign Affairs Committee that the U.S. and South Korean governments both believe that North Korea was responsible for this attack.[429]

2. 2014: Suspected Cyberattack on South Korean Nuclear Power Plants

In December 2014, hackers attacked South Korea's Korea Hydro & Nuclear Power, Ltd. (KHNP) with malware and released blueprints for multiple South Korean nuclear power plants. A South Korean joint government investigation team led by the Seoul Central District Prosecutors' Office traced the cyberattack to the Chinese city of Shenyang, a location in which North Korean hackers are known to operate. According to a report in *The Joongang Daily*, "the hackers' group threatened that the three nuclear reactors in Gori and Wolseong must be shut down by Christmas or they would reveal more files and carry out a second attack," and threatened that "[i]t will be a Fukushima."[430]

The investigation team concluded that the attack was carefully planned. Although South Korean Justice Minister Hwang Kyo-ahn told the National Assembly that authorities were investigating suspicions that North Korea may have been behind the attack, an official from the investigation team said, "We cannot confirm nor deny the North's involvement in the case." The South Korean

426   Choe Sang-hun, "Computer Networks in South Korea Are Paralyzed in Cyberattacks," *op. cit.*

427   In-soo Nam and Alastair Gale, "Seoul Investigates Web Shutdown," *The Wall Street Journal*, 20 March 2013.

428   The Dark Seoul attack also coincided with a cyberattack against HRNK (*See* Choe Sang-hun, "Computer Networks in South Korea Are Paralyzed in Cyberattacks," *op. cit.*). According to HRNK's Executive Director, Greg Scarlatoiu, the hackers "vandalized both the English and Korean HRNK websites." It was not clear whether the attack was linked to those in South Korea, or whether evidence linked the attack to North Korea.

429   "North Korea Threat Assessment," *C-SPAN*, 13 January 2015, http://www.c-span.org/video/?323725-1/hearing-north-korean-cyber-nuclear-threats.

430   Jung Hyo-sik and Ser Myo-ja, "North suspected in nuke hacking," *Korea JoongAng Daily*, 26 December 2014.

government asked the Chinese government to cooperate with its investigation and prevent further cyberattacks from its territory. In March 2015, the South Korean government publicly accused North Korea of responsibility for the attack. According to the South Korean government, the investigation team found that "the hackers intended to cause a malfunction at atomic reactors, but failed to break into their control system" and carried out the attack "to stir up social unrest and agitation in our country." South Korea's Unification Ministry condemned the attack as "cyber-terror targeting our country and the international community," and accused Pyongyang of "taking the life and safety of our people as a hostage."[431]

3. 2014: Cyberattacks against Sony Pictures Entertainment Inc., and Threats Against American Moviegoers

Although North Korea's threats against the feature film "The Interview" did not attract widespread attention until December of 2014, *KCNA* published its first threat against the film in June:

DPRK FM Spokesman Blasts U.S. Moves to Hurt Dignity of Supreme Leadership of DPRK

Pyongyang, June 25 (KCNA) -- The spokesman for the Foreign Ministry of the DPRK released the following statement Wednesday:

The enemies have gone beyond the tolerance limit in their despicable moves to dare hurt the dignity of the supreme leadership of the DPRK.

A preview of a film on insulting and assassinating the supreme leadership of the DPRK is floating in broad daylight in the U.S., a kingpin of international terrorism and its cesspool, shocking the world community.

The U.S. has gone reckless in such provocative hysteria as bribing a rogue movie maker to dare hurt the dignity of the supreme leadership of the DPRK. This act of not fearing any punishment from Heaven is touching off the towering hatred and wrath of the service personnel and people of the DPRK.

---

431   "South Korea Accuses North of Cyber-attacks on Nuclear Plants," *AFP*, 17 March 2015.

The above-said practice is, however, a revelation of its fear as it is taken aback by the bright and rosy future of the DPRK under the leadership of the peerless great man and a last-ditch effort of those who are seized by a daydream.

Absolutely intolerable is the distribution of such film in the U.S. as it is the most undisguised terrorism and a war action to deprive the service personnel and people of the DPRK of their mental mainstay and bring down its social system.

The dignified and worthwhile life the Korean people enjoy at present and the great changes taking place in the country as well as everything valuable that will belong to the rosy future when the dreams and ideals of the people will come true would be unthinkable apart from the supreme leadership of the DPRK.

That's why they regard the supreme leadership as dearer than their own lives.

It is their firm determination and stamina to mercilessly destroy anyone who dares hurt or attack the supreme leadership of the country even a bit.

Those who defamed our supreme leadership and committed the hostile acts against the DPRK can never escape the stern punishment to be meted out according to a law wherever they might be in the world.

If the U.S. administration connives at and patronizes the screening of the film, it will invite a strong and merciless countermeasure.[432]

The New York Times later reported that, as a consequence of this threat, an executive of Sony Pictures Entertainment Inc. Japan "intervened in the decision making of his company's usually autonomous Hollywood studio" and demanded changes to a scene depicting the death of Kim Jong-un, over the objections of the film's director, Seth Rogen.[433]

---

432   "DPRK FM Spokesman Blasts U.S. Moves to Hurt Dignity of Supreme Leadership of DPRK," *KCNA*, 25 June 2014.

433   Martin Fackler, Brooks Barnes and David E. Sanger, "Sony's International Incident: Making Kim Jong-un's Head Explode," *The New York Times*, 14 December 2014.

On the morning of Monday, November 24th, Sony Pictures Entertainment Inc. employees who arrived at work turned on their computers to an image of "a sneering red skeleton" and the message, "Hacked By #GOP," or Guardians of Peace. Then, Sony Pictures Entertainment Inc.'s system "went dark."[434] Later that day, the Guardians of Peace began to release sensitive Sony Pictures Entertainment Inc. information, including financial and personal information about its employees, and the e-mails of Sony Pictures Entertainment Inc. executives.[435] Some news sources printed the e-mails, which contained candid (and sometimes embarrassing) statements their authors had made during confidential discussions.

Almost immediately, there was speculation that North Korea was behind the Guardians of Peace attack,[436] but it was not until early December that news reports began to cite[437] federal investigators who blamed[438] North Korean hackers operating[439] from Chinese soil.[440] On December 6th, North Korea denied responsibility for the attack, but called it "a righteous deed."[441]

---

434   Ryan Faughnder, Paresh Dave and Saba Hamedy, "Hack at Sony Pictures shuts computer system," *Los Angeles Times*, 24 November 2014.

435   Saba Hamedy, "Sony hackers issue threat in latest message: 'The world will be full of fear'," *Los Angeles Times*, 16 December 2014.

436   "Sony looks for possible North Korea link in hacking incident: report," *Reuters*, 29 November 2014.

437   Danny Yadron and Ben Fritz, "More Signs North Korea May Be Behind Hacking of Sony Pictures," *The Wall Street Journal*, 02 December 2014.

438   Ellen Nakashima, Craig Timberg and Andrea Peterson, "Sony Pictures hack appears to be linked to North Korea, investigators say," *The Washington Post*, 03 December 2014.

439   Arik Hesseldahl, "Sony Pictures Investigates North Korea Link In Hack Attack," *Re/code*, 28 November 2014.

440   A 2009 paper by then-U.S. Army Major Steve Sin alleged that North Korean hackers operated from the North Korean-owned Chilbosan Hotel in the city of Shenyang (*See* Steve Sin, "Cyber Threat posed by North Korea and China to South Korea and US Forces Korea" (May 2009), 5; James Cook, "Inside The Luxury Chinese Hotel Where North Korea Keeps Its Army of Hackers," *Business Insider*, 02 December 2014). In an interview with *CNN* on January 7, 2015, Sin stated his belief that, according to "the best information available to us," North Korean hackers continue to operate from Shenyang (Will Ripley, "North Korean defector: 'Bureau 121' hackers operating in China," *CNN*, 07 January 2015).

441   Anna Fifield, "North Korea denies hacking Sony but calls the breach a 'righteous deed'," *The Washington Post*, 07 December 2014.

On the morning of December 16th, the Guardians of Peace sent the following message to Sony Pictures Entertainment Inc.:

Warning

We will clearly show it to you at the very time and places "The Interview" be shown, including the premiere, how bitter fate those who seek fun in terror should be doomed to.

Soon all the world will see what an awful movie Sony Pictures Entertainment has made.

The world will be full of fear.

Remember the 11th of September 2001.

We recommend you to keep yourself distant from the places at that time.

(If your house is nearby, you'd better leave.)

Whatever comes in the coming days is called by the greed of Sony Pictures Entertainment.

All the world will denounce the SONY.

More to come...[442]

---

442   Brent Lang, "Sony Hackers Threaten 9/11 Attack on Movie Theaters That Screen 'The Interview,'" *Variety*, 16 December 2014.

On December 17th, Sony Pictures Entertainment Inc. canceled the film's release.[443] The same day, New Regency[444] announced[445] that it would scrap a second film about North Korea.[446] The decisions caused a public reaction by some observers, who accused the studios of yielding to threats. In Hollywood, George Clooney[447] and Rob Lowe[448] were harshly critical of Sony Pictures Entertainment Inc.'s decision. President Obama said he wished that Sony Pictures Entertainment Inc. had asked him first: "I would have told them, 'Do not get into a pattern where you get intimidated by these criminal attacks.'"[449] In late December, Sony Pictures Entertainment Inc. reversed its decision and released "The Interview" in a limited number of theaters and online.[450]

The same day, *The New York Times* reported that federal investigators had concluded that North Korea was "centrally involved" in the cyberattack, and that the White House was debating whether to announce this conclusion publicly.[451] The *Times* wrote that Japan opposed this, fearing "that a public accusation could interfere with delicate diplomatic negotiations for the return of Japanese citizens kidnapped years ago."[452] More than 20 years after the kidnappings, the abduction issue continues to complicate U.S.-Japan relations.

443   Rebecca Ford, "Sony Cancels Release of 'The Interview'," *The Hollywood Reporter*, 17 December 2014.

444   Mike Fleming Jr., "North Korea-Based Thriller With Gore Verbinski And Steve Carell Canceled," *Deadline*, 17 December 2014.

445   Dave McNary, "Steve Carell's North Korea-Set Project Dropped by New Regency," *Variety*, 17 December 2014.

446   Jeff Sneider, "Steve Carell's North Korea Movie 'Pyongyang' Canceled in Wake of Sony Hack," *The Wrap*, 17 December 2014.

447   Breeanna Hare, "George Clooney: We need to stand with Sony," *CNN*, 19 December 2014.

448   Adam Withnall, "The Interview: Rob Lowe says Sony cancelling Kim Jong-Un assassination film is like Europe giving in to Hitler," *The Independent*, 18 December 2014.

449   Mark Berman, "Live updates: Obama press conference - Sony 'made a mistake'," *The Washington Post*, 19 December 2014.

450   Gregory Wallace and Brian Stelter, "Sony: What theaters are showing 'The Interview' on Christmas Day," *CNN Money*, 24 December 2014.

451   David E. Sanger and Nicole Perlroth, "U.S. Said to Find North Korea Ordered Cyberattack on Sony," *The New York Times*, 17 December 2014.

452   Hyperlink in original to: Martin Fackler, "North Korea Will Investigate Fate of Abducted Japanese," *The New York Times*, 29 May 2014.

On December 19, 2014, the FBI issued a statement accusing the government of North Korea of being behind the Guardians of Peace cyberattack and threat.[453] Later that day, President Obama commented on the FBI's findings and their implications for freedom of expression in the United States:

> "We cannot have a society in which some dictator someplace can start imposing censorship here in the United States," Obama said. "Because if somebody is able to intimidate folks out of releasing a satirical movie, imagine what they start doing when they see a documentary that they don't like or news reports that they don't like."[454]

The President promised to "respond proportionally" to the attack.[455] In Congress, there were new calls to return North Korea to the SSOT list, including from the outgoing Democratic Chairman of the Senate Foreign Relations Committee, Sen. Bob Menendez,[456] and from the Chairwoman of the House Subcommittee on the Middle East and North Africa, Rep. Ileana Ros-Lehtinen.[457]

On December 20, 2014, North Korea again denied any involvement in the cyberattack, and denied threatening to attack theaters where "The Interview" would be screened, but publicly threatened the makers of the film again:

> We will never pardon those undesirable elements keen on hurting the dignity of the supreme leadership of the DPRK. In case we retaliate against them, we will target with legitimacy those responsible for the anti-DPRK acts and their bases, not engaging in terrorist attack aimed at the innocent audience in cinemas.

---

453   Federal Bureau of Investigation, "Update on Sony Investigation," 19 December 2014.

454   Ellen Nakashima, "U.S. attributes cyberattack on Sony to North Korea," *The Washington Post*, 19 December 2014.

455   *See* U.S. DEP'T OF ARMY, OPERATIONAL LAW HANDBOOK 4 (2014) ("To comply with the proportionality criterion, States must limit the magnitude, scope, and duration of any use of force to that level of force which is reasonably necessary to counter a threat or attack").

456   "Press Release: Chairman Menendez Writes Secretary Kerry on North Korea's Cyber-Terror Attack on Sony Pictures," *Bob Menendez for New Jersey*, 19 December 2014, http://www.menendez.senate.gov/news-and-events/press/chairman-menendez-writes-secretary-kerry-on-north-koreas-cyber-terror-attack-on-sony-pictures.

457   "U.S. congresswoman vows bill listing N.K. as terror sponsor," *Yonhap News*, 06 January 2015.

The army of the DPRK has the will and ability to do so.[458]

On January 2, 2015, President Obama signed an executive order authorizing broader sanctions against North Korea, its ruling party, and its officials, but blocked the assets of just 10 individuals and three previously designated entities. The executive order cited several reasons for the new sanctions, including North Korea's "destructive, coercive cyber-related actions during November and December 2014."[459]

Some private security firms questioned North Korea's responsibility for the attacks, suggesting that a disgruntled Sony Pictures Entertainment Inc. employee may have been responsible instead.[460] The White House, the FBI,[461] and the National Security Agency[462] continue to express their confidence that North Korea carried out the attack.[463] An unnamed intelligence official told *The Washington Post* that officials involved in the investigation "know very specifically who the attackers are."[464]

North Korea has since embarked on a global campaign to suppress "The Interview." On January 16th, *The New York Times* reported that North Korean diplomats demanded that Burmese authorities seize all copies of "The Interview."[465] *Variety* later reported that North Korean diplomats demanded the removal of "The Interview" from the Berlin Film Festival, stating:[466]

---

458   "DPRK Foreign Ministry Rejects U.S. Accusation against Pyongyang over Cyber Attack," *KCNA*, 20 December 2014.

459   Exec. Order 13,687, 80 Fed. Reg. 817 (Jan. 06, 2015).

460   "New evidence Sony hack was 'inside' job, not North Korea," *New York Post*, 30 December 2014.

461   Michael S. Schmidt, Nicole Perlroth and Matthew Goldstein, "F.B.I. Says Little Doubt North Korea Hit Sony," *The New York Times*, 07 January 2015.

462   David E. Sanger and Martin Fackler, "N.S.A. Breached North Korean Networks Before Sony Attack, Officials Say," *The New York Times*, 18 January 2015.

463   Andrew Grossman, "U.S. Confident on North Korea Involvement in Sony Threats," *The Wall Street Journal*, 07 January 2015.

464   Ellen Nakashima, "White House says Sony hack is a serious national security matter," *The Washington Post*, 18 December 2014.

465   Wai Moe and Choe Sang-hun, "Myanmar Sweeps Up Copies of Film Mocking Kim Jong-un," *The New York Times*, 16 January 2015.

466   Leo Barraclough, "North Korea, Berlin Film Festival Clear Up Mix-Up Over 'The Interview'," *Variety*, 22 January 2015.

The U.S. and Germany should immediately stop the farce of screening anti-DPRK movie at the film festival. Those who attempt at terrorist acts and commit politically-motivated provocations and those who join them in violation of the sovereignty and dignity of the DPRK will never be able to escape merciless punishment.[467]

The demand arose from North Korea's mistaken belief that "The Interview" was to be exhibited at the festival; it was not.[468] "The Interview" was coincidentally scheduled to open in German theaters on February 5th, the same day that the festival would begin. On January 25th, The *Bangkok Post* reported that North Korea had asked Cambodia to ban sales of "The Interview."[469]

North Korea's threat against "The Interview" is not North Korea's first threat against the United States, but it is the most effective threat ever used by a foreign power to chill free expression in the United States and in other countries. The *L.A. Times* reports that the cyberattack and threat cost Sony Pictures Entertainment Inc. "tens of millions of dollars." At least one other film project was canceled in its early stages.[470] The chilling effects of the cyberattack and threat on other film studios, publishers, artists, and journalists are hard to assess.[471]

4. ANALYSIS

To the extent a hacker communicates a threat of violence, using an explosive or other dangerous device, with the intent to endanger the safety of one or more individuals, the threat would fit the plain meaning of "terrorism" and the definition of "terrorist activity" at INA § 212(a)(3)(B) (iii).[472] To the extent the threat originated from subnational groups or clandestine agents—in

---

467   "U.S., Germany Urged to Give Up at Once Screening of Anti-DPRK Movie: DPRK FM Spokesman," *KCNA*, 21 January 2015 (archived at the author's blog: "Then they came for the Germans: N. Korea's global censorship campaign," *One Free Korea*, 26 January 2015).

468   Ben Child, "Confused North Korea accuses Berlin film festival of 'terrorism'," *The Guardian*, 23 January 2015.

469   "Cambodia asked to ban 'The Interview'," *the Bangkok Post*, 25 January 2015.

470   Meg James, Daniel Miller and Josh Rottenberg, "Sony Pictures execs debated risk of 'The Interview' before cyberattack," *Los Angeles Times*, 09 December 2014.

471   Ann Oldenburg, "Steve Carell movie set in North Korea is nixed," *USA Today*, 18 December 2014.

472   Immigration and Nationality Act, Pub. L. No. 82-414, § 212(a)(3)(B)(ii) added by Pub. L. No. 101-649, § 601(a), 104 Stat. 5067 (as amended by Pub. L. No. 107-56, § 411(a)(1), 115 Stat. 345).

this case, hackers acting under the command of the RGB — it would also fit the FRAA Section 140 definition, as the U.S. State Department has historically interpreted it to include threats of "premeditated, politically motivated" violence against noncombatants (*supra* Section III.E.3). The threat against "The Interview" was a threat to commit a criminal, violent act across international boundaries, to both intimidate and coerce a civilian population, and as such, could be prosecuted as "international terrorism" under Chapter 113B of the U.S. Criminal Code.[473] Thus, the threat against audiences for "The Interview" qualifies as "international terrorism" and would support a SSOT re-listing of North Korea.

The cyberattack against Sony Pictures Entertainment Inc., however, would not meet these standards. It does not meet the FRAA Section 140 definition of "international terrorism," because it was not a "violent" attack. Similarly, it would not meet the Criminal Code's definition of "international terrorism" at 18 U.S.C. § 2331(1) unless it could be considered a "violent act." Section 16 of the Criminal Code defines the term "crime of violence" as "an offense that has as an element the use, attempted use, or threatened use of physical force against the person or property of another."[474] It would only fit the definition of "terrorist activity" at INA § 212(a)(3)(B)(iii) if it involved the use of a "dangerous device."[475] One could argue that defining malware as a "dangerous device" serves sound national security interests, but without statutory clarification, most courts would be unwilling to leave so much discretion to the prosecutorial imagination. A similar analysis would apply to the North Korean cyberattacks of 2009 to 2013.

Despite the prevalence of the term "cyberterrorism" — a term that is neither used nor defined in the Criminal Code — the U.S. State Department has never cited a cyberattack as a basis for a SSOT listing.[476] At the same time, it is also clear that cyberattacks can be dangerous to property and human life, if one considers, for example, cyberattacks against nuclear power plants.[477]

---

473   18 U.S.C. § 2331.

474   18 U.S.C. § 16.

475   Immigration and Nationality Act, Pub. L. No. 82-414, § 212(a)(3)(B)(ii) added by Pub. L. No. 101-649, § 601(a), 104 Stat. 5067 (as amended by Pub. L. No. 107-56, § 411(a)(1), 115 Stat. 345).

476   Some media sources attribute the following definition of the term "cyber-terrorism" to the FBI: "A premeditated, politically motivated attack against information, computer systems, computer programs and data which results in violence against non-combatant targets by sub-national groups or clandestine agents." The author found no original source for this definition in any materials published by the FBI.

477   Elisabeth Bumiller and Thom Shanker, "Panetta Warns of Dire Threat of Cyberattacks on U.S.," *The New York Times*, 11 October 2012.

The cyberattack against KHNP could meet the legal definition of support for international terrorism. Although the South Korean investigation team had not released detailed findings about the attack at the time of publication of this report, a cyberattack causing physical damage to the plant, or endangering human life or safety, would be a violent and dangerous act. The circumstances suggest that the attack was premeditated, and the hackers made multiple contacts with KHNP between December 2014 and March 2015. The South Korean investigation concluded that the attack had a political motive. The hackers' modus operandi is similar to that of Unit 121, a clandestine unit of the RGB. Although the attack did not succeed in damaging the reactor, endangering human life, or causing social unrest in South Korea, there is ample precedent for classifying attempts as terrorist attacks (*supra* Section II.E.3).

VI. CONCLUSION AND RECOMMENDATIONS

Since 2006, when the U.S. State Department first expressed its intention to remove North Korea from the SSOT list, North Korea's sponsorship of terrorism has increased in terms of its seriousness, frequency, and global reach.

Congress created the authority to list a state as a sponsor of terrorism to deter the offending sponsorship, but Congress's deterrent purpose can only be served if the executive branch, which is charged with enforcing and administering the laws, does so as Congress intended. Although the U.S. State Department often suggests that the legal standards for a SSOT listing are rigorous and confining, in reality, the standard is vague and malleable, requiring no more than the Secretary of State's determination that the state has repeatedly provided support for acts of international terrorism. The law applies no more precise standard, procedure for listing, or accepted definition of the term "international terrorism." All that is necessary is for the U.S. State Department to acknowledge the evidence and apply it to the law, in the same manner that it has applied the law to Iran, Syria, and other countries.

A. CLARIFY THE LEGAL STANDARDS FOR SSOT LISTING

The vagueness of the current standards for SSOT listing requires the analyst to consult multiple legal definitions and many years of precedent to judge whether a given act qualifies as the sponsorship of international terrorism. Even then, the definitions and precedents conflict; consequently, the answers are often unclear. A single pattern of conduct may lend itself to different interpretations, depending on one's policy objectives. For the SSOT listing process to serve its intended deterrent purposes, it must put international actors on notice of what conduct is classifiable and sanctionable as the sponsorship of international terrorism.

1. Clarify the Definition of "International Terrorism"

Congress should enact a single, clear definition of "international terrorism" in the Export Administration Act that is consistent with accepted meanings of that term. By placing the definition within the Act, Congress will clarify that the definition applies for purposes of a SSOT listing. None of the existing definitions are clearly better than the others. The definition in FRAA Section 140 fails to clarify that threats of terrorism are also terrorism, or the requisite intent that qualifies a violent act as an act of terrorism. The definition in INA § 212(a)(3)(B)(iii) is convoluted,[478] and like the definition in 18 U.S.C. § 2331(1), is overbroad in that it fails to limit its reach to acts by subnational groups or clandestine agents. A clearer definition could read as follows:

§2415. Definitions

As used in this Act [sections 2401 to 2420 of this Appendix]— ...

(9) the term "international terrorism" means any act that—

> (A) is unlawful under the laws of the place where it is committed;

> (B) involves a violent act; an act dangerous to human life, property, or infrastructure; or a threat of such an act;

> (C) involves the citizens or the territory of more than one country;

> (D) is perpetrated by a subnational group or clandestine agent against a noncombatant target; and

> (E) appears to be intended to intimidate or coerce a civilian population; to influence the policy of a government by intimidation or coercion; or to affect the conduct of a government.

Congress could clarify the standards for SSOT listing further by harmonizing the definition in FRAA Section 140 to conform to this language, by cross-referencing this definition in the statutes that legislate the consequences of an SSOT listing (*supra* Section II.F), and by defining the term "noncombatant."

---

478   Immigration and Nationality Act, Pub. L. No. 82-414, § 212(a)(3)(B)(ii) added by Pub. L. No. 101-649, § 601(a), 104 Stat. 5067 (as amended by Pub. L. No. 107-56, § 411(a)(1), 115 Stat. 345).

This language has the additional advantage that it would more easily apply to cyberattacks that involve violence or danger to human life.

2. CLARIFY THE DEFINITION OF "SUPPORT"

Because no statute defines what constitutes "support" for international terrorism, the analyst must choose between inferring that the confusing and incoherent reporting standards in FRAA Section 140 are an operational definition of support, relying on the U.S. State Department's inconsistent reporting on the state sponsorship of terrorism, or relying on the non-binding language of a 1989 congressional report. As applied by the U.S. State Department, "support" has historically included both material support for terrorist organizations and clandestine terrorist acts by state actors. A definition consistent with this meaning could read as follows:

§2415. Definitions

As used in this Act [sections 2401 to 2420 of this Appendix]— ...

(10) the term "support for international terrorism" means—

> (A) to solicit or direct a terrorist, a subnational group, or a clandestine agent to commit an act of international terrorism;

> (B) to provide material support, as such term is defined in Section 2339A(b) of Title 18, U.S. Code, to an international terrorist or a Foreign Terrorist Organization; or

> (C) to attempt, facilitate, conspire to commit, or threaten to commit any of the conduct described in paragraphs (A) or (B).

The U.S. State and Treasury Departments could further clarify this definition by adopting a single authoritative definition of "terrorist organization" for purposes of designating Foreign Terrorist Organizations, and for designations under Executive Order 13,224 (*supra* Section II.B). Alternatively, Congress could adopt a definition of "terrorist organization" that disjunctively includes the persons and entities designated under both authorities.

Joshua Stanton

3. Report and Consider All Acts that Meet the Legal Standards

The SSOT list cannot serve the deterrent purpose Congress intended unless the U.S. State Department reports the relevant facts truthfully and follows them to logical conclusions. For example, the assertion that North Korea has not sponsored any acts of terrorism since 1987 is no longer defensible. Whatever the legal or policy merits of a SSOT designation, the American people have a right to expect their government to speak candidly and truthfully about matters that are important for public and foreign policy.

Congress could remedy the U.S. State Department's selective reporting of support for international terrorism by amending FRAA Section 140, to allow Congress to require the U.S. State Department to report on acts that may constitute support for acts of international terrorism. Such an amendment could allow the Chairman of the Senate Foreign Relations Committee or the Chairman of the House Foreign Affairs Committee to notify the Secretary of State when the Chair has reasonable grounds to believe that a government has provided support for an act of international terrorism. The notification would then require the U.S. State Department to determine, in its next annual "Country Reports," whether the act qualifies as support for international terrorism under the clarified definition of that term. A notification would also require the Secretary of State to determine whether the government had provided support for an act of international terrorism before the SSOT rescission process in Section 6(j)(4) of the Export Administration Act could become final.

B. Create an Alternative Authority to Sanction Threats to International Peace that Are Not Sponsorship of Terrorism

The proliferation of weapons of mass destruction is clearly one of the world's greatest security challenges. It is equally clear that no evidence links some of the most dangerous acts of proliferation, such as the construction of the Al-Kibar reactor and the use of chemical weapons in Syria, to international terrorism. The U.S. State Department's current practice is to report—selectively—the development and proliferation of weapons of mass destruction as part of its annual reporting on terrorism, even when the links between proliferation and terrorism are tenuous and speculative. This further confuses the definition and deterrence of the sponsorship of terrorism.

The expansive interpretation of "support for acts of international terrorism" may arise from a recognition that a remedy similar to the SSOT list is also needed in other compelling circumstances. The sponsorship of terrorism is only one category of conduct that threatens international peace and compels the use of powerful legal deterrents. Similar deterrents could also apply to unprovoked attacks on U.S. treaty allies, threats of attacks against civilian targets, cyberattacks, and crimes against humanity—categories of conduct that do not necessarily include support for acts of international terrorism. Congress could describe these categories of conduct as what they are—whether individually, or collectively, as threats to global peace. By creating powerful legal remedies for such conduct, Congress could reduce the political pressure on policymakers to support military responses to it instead.

If Congress were to authorize a separate list of states that threaten international peace, it could apply any of the sanctions described in Section II.F or Section VI.C of this report to states designated as threats to international peace. If Congress were to create such an authority, North Korea would be a strong candidate for designation.

C. Reconsider the Sufficiency of Existing SSOT Sanctions

To the extent that the U.S. State Department argues that a SSOT listing is merely "symbolic," this is not as much an argument against the SSOT listing of North Korea, as it is an argument that the consequences of an SSOT listing are insufficient to serve their intended deterrent purpose. Congress could remedy this deficiency by legislating additional consequences for SSOT-listed states, including one or more of the following:

- reenactment of the paragraph in the 1985 amendment to Section 620A of the Foreign Assistance Act, which called on the President to "call upon other countries to impose similar sanctions on" SSOT-listed governments;

- increased financial sanctions against SSOT-listed states, including the restriction of access to the international financial system by governments that sponsor terrorism, including by applying financial special measures to jurisdictions designated as SSOTs;[479]

- increased financial sanctions against specific government entities responsible for terrorist threats and attacks, such as the Reconnaissance General Bureau of the Workers' Party[480] and *KCNA*, and their key officials;

---

479   31 U.S.C. § 5318A.

480   The Reconnaissance General Bureau's property and assets are already blocked under multiple executive orders. *See* http://www.treasury.gov/ofac/downloads/.

- calling for the designation of the Reconnaissance General Bureau under Executive Order 13,224, thereby identifying it with international terrorism, similar to the IGRC-Quds Force;

- enacting new secondary sanctions against governments that fail to inspect cargo originating in SSOT-listed states; and

- enacting new requirements for securities issuers to disclose any investments in SSOT-listed states in their public filings with the Securities and Exchange Commission.

North Korea's sponsorship of terrorism has become a serious global human rights concern—for human rights activists, refugees, and dissidents-in-exile; for civilians in third countries, like Japan and Israel; for journalists and civilians in South Korea; and now, for artists and audiences in the United States who wish to exercise their rights to free expression. There is an important public interest in protecting the rights of those who are being terrorized, hurt, and killed by North Korea's conduct. It is past time for the Secretary of State to carefully review North Korea's past and recent conduct and to recognize that North Korea has repeatedly provided support for acts of international terrorism.